Virgil, *Aeneid* 6

OCR GCSE Selection for 2023 and 2024

Lines 295-316, 384-416, 679-712, 752-759, 788-800

A Tiered Reader

By Sam Koon and Helena Walters

Disclaimer:

This book is in no way affiliated with, or endorsed by OCR.

Preface

The aim of this book is to help make Virgil's poetry more comprehensible. As such, it includes tiered readings for all of the Virgil set text to be examined at GCSE in 2023 and 2024 (OCR).

Each section has three tiers: a simple version, an ORDO, and Virgil's text itself.

At GCSE (and beyond) Latin students need to be able to discuss 'content', 'word choice' and 'word position' or 'style'. Each of the tiers is designed to help students better understand Virgil's poetry in these three areas.

The first tier is a simplified version which describes what is happening in easy Latin. Not only does this allow students to read more Latin, the first tier can be read independently to ensure students have a strong knowledge of the whole set text (which is examined in the final 10 marker of the GCSE).

The second tier is an ORDO version of the text: Virgil's words in English prose order. This allows pupils to focus on Virgil's word choice in comparison to the first tier, which uses high frequency words.

The final tier is Virgil's original. This tier allows pupils, now comfortable with the content and vocabulary, to appreciate Virgil's style and comment on where he has chosen to place his words.

In addition, at the end of each section there are a number of questions and discussion points designed to help pupils better understand the set text and prepare for the examination.

Introduction to the Text

Today we call Augustus the 'first' emperor of Rome. However, when he came to power in 27 BC, no one knew that he would rule for the rest of his life, let alone that his descendants would rule after him.

Augustus gained sole control of Rome after decades of civil wars. Several men had tried to lead Rome on their own, including Augustus' own adoptive father, Julius Caesar, who had been murdered in a rebellion against his rule in 44 BC.

Augustus wanted to avoid this fate and keep control of the empire. He was brutal to his enemies but also used 'softer' methods. He wanted to convince the Roman people that his rule would lead to a new golden age: a time of peace and success for the Roman people after so much violence and disruption. For example, he changed his own name from Octavius to Augustus (meaning the 'holy' man). He also began a huge rebuilding programme in Rome, carrying out many projects, such as the construction of new aqueducts to improve the water supply, that couldn't be attempted while Rome was at war.

Augustus also used culture as part of this programme. He gathered a group of talented writers and rewarded them for producing great poems worthy of the new Rome. Of course, it helped if they praised Augustus in their writing!

Virgil was one of these poets. His plan was to write an epic poem in Latin that was as good as - or better - than the famous Greek epic poems by Homer. For a long time Romans had admired Greek poems and wanted to have something just as good written in Latin.

The Aeneid tells the story of a single man who successfully leads his people to peace after many years of war. Augustus certainly saw lots of similarities between himself and the hero Aeneas. Today, people disagree about whether Virgil intended the Aeneid to praise Augustus.

The Story of Aeneas

Aeneas appears as a minor character in the *Iliad*, the Greek epic poem that inspired Virgil. He is the son of the goddess Aphrodite (Venus to the Romans) and a Trojan prince, Anchises. Aeneas fights on the Trojan side in the war with the Greeks. However, the Trojans lose and Troy falls. Aeneas escapes carrying his father, holding his son Ascanius' hand and saving some of Troy's religious objects. This moment represents the quality for which he is most famous: his *pietas* (duty towards family, state and gods). Aeneas' wife, Creusa, is separated from the group and dies in Troy.

Aeneas gathers the remaining Trojan refugees and sets off by sea to find somewhere to build a new city. This proves to be difficult and after multiple false starts and obscure prophecies, Aeneas learns that his destiny is to found a great city in Italy (Rome).

While sailing towards Italy, Aeneas' ships are blown off course by a storm created by Juno, Queen of the gods, who hates Aeneas because he is a Trojan. Aeneas is shipwrecked on the coast near the new city of Carthage

Lines 295-316: Charon and the way to the underworld

295-297: The Road to Tartarus

Tier 1

Haec est via ad fluvium Acherontem.

Fluvius Acheron est in Tartaro.

Tartarus est terra mortuorum.

Hic est <u>gurges</u> (an abyss) plenus <u>caeno</u> (with filth/mud).

Haec est vasta <u>vorago</u> (whirlpool).

Haec vorago iacit <u>harenam</u> (sand) in fluvium Cocytum.

ORDO

Hinc via, quae fert ad undas Tartarei Acherontis.

hic gurges turbidus caeno -que vasta voragine aestuat,

atque eructat omnem harenam Cocyto.

Carmen ipsum

Hinc via Tartarei quae fert Acherontis ad undas.   295

turbidus hic caeno vastaque voragine gurges

aestuat atque omnem Cocyto eructat harenam.

Questions *Aeneid* 6.295-297

1. How does Virgil make the road to Tartarus seem intimidating?

   Quote Latin that supports your answer.

2. Identify two rhetorical devices in these lines

3. Research *Tartarus*, *Acheron* and *Cocytus*. Write a

   one-sentence description for each.

298-308: Charon the Ferryman

Tier 1

Charon est <u>portitor</u> (ferryman).

portitor servat fluvium.

Charon non est pulcher sed sordidus et terribilis.

Charon habet barbam albam.

Charon barbam albam non servat.

oculi Charontis sunt flammae.

Charon gerit <u>amictum</u> (cloak).

amictus quoque sordidus est.

amictus ex umeris pendet.

Charon <u>ratem</u> (raft) agit cum <u>conto</u> (pole) et <u>velis</u> (sails).

Charon portat corpora in rate.

ratis est color sanguinis antiqui

Charon est antiquus sed est deus. dei antiqui sunt fortes.

multi mortui ad fluvium veniunt: feminae, viri, heroes, pueri, puellae
et iuvenes.

ORDO

Portitor Charon, horrendus terribile squalore,

servat has aquas et flumina,

cui plurima canities iacet inculta mento,

lumina stant flamma,

sordidus amictus [in] nodo de-pendet ex umeris.

ipse subigit ratem conto, -que ministrat velis,

et subvectat corpora ferruginea cymba,

iam senior, sed cruda -que viridis senectus deo.

huc omnis turba effusa ruebat ad ripas;

matres atque viri,

-que corpora magnanimum heroum defuncta vita,

pueri -que innuptae puellae,

-que iuvenes impositi [in] rogis [= in flammis] ante ora parentum:

Carmen ipsum

portitor has horrendus aquas et flumina servat

terribili squalore Charon, cui plurima mento

canities inculta iacet, stant lumina flamma,   300

sordidus ex umeris nodo dependet amictus.

ipse ratem conto subigit velisque ministrat

et ferruginea subvectat corpora cymba,

iam senior, sed cruda deo viridisque senectus.

huc omnis turba ad ripas effusa ruebat,   305

matres atque viri defunctaque corpora vita

magnanimum heroum, pueri innuptaeque puellae,

impositique rogis iuvenes ante ora parentum:

Questions *Aeneid* 6.298-308

1. How is Charon presented? Make five points and quote the
   Latin to support your answer.

2. In lines 305-308, how does Virgil emphasise the sheer number
   of souls at the river bank?

3. In which more modern stories, films or books, have you seen
   Charon depicted?

4. Draw a sketch of Charon and annotate it in Latin.

309-316: Two similes describing the crowd of souls

Tier 1

Tempora anni sunt quattuor: ver, aestas, autumnus et hiems.

Autumnus est tempus a mense Septembri ad Novembrem.

Autumnus est frigidus.

In silvis sunt multi arbores.

Ubi autumnus est frigidus, multa folia (leaves) in silvis cadunt.

Multae aves (birds) conveniunt et ab oceano ad terram volant,

Ubi frigidus annus eas trans pontem pellit

Et eas ad calidam terram mittit.

Multi mortui in ripa (river bank) stabant.

Multi mortui dicunt: "volumus transire!"

Sed tristis navita nunc accipit hos mortuos

et nunc accipt illos mortuos

Sed tristis navita arcet (wards off) alios mortuos.

ORDO

quam multa folia lapsa cadunt in silvis primo frigore autumni,

aut quam multae aves glomerantur ab alto gurgite,

ubi frigidus annus fugat trans pontem,

et immittit [eas] apricis terris.

Stabant orantes transmittere cursum primi,

-que tendebant manus amore ulterioris ripae;

sed tristis navita nunc accipit hos, nunc illos,

ast arcet alios longe summotos harena.

Carmen ipsum

quam multa in silvis autumni frigore primo

lapsa cadunt folia, aut ad terram gurgite ab alto   310

quam multae glomerantur aves, ubi frigidus annus

trans pontum fugat et terris immittit apricis.

stabant orantes primi transmittere cursum

tendebantque manus ripae ulterioris amore.

navita sed tristis nunc hos nunc accipit illos,   315

ast alios longe summotos arcet harena.

Questions on *Aeneid* 6.309-316

1. Analyse the two similes. What is their purpose?

2. How does Virgil emphasise the pathos of this scene? Make 5
   points and quote the Latin to support your answer.

Lines 384-416: The Golden Bough and crossing the Styx

384-387: Charon spies the mortals

Tier 1

Ergo Aeneas et Sibylla iter faciunt at ad fluvium eunt.

Charon est <u>navita</u> (sailor).

Navita in media Stygia est.

Navita eos ab Stygia spectat.

Aeneas et Sibylla per <u>tacitum nemus</u> (the silent grove) eunt.

Nunc Navita spectat eos ire per tacitum nemus.

Aeneas et Sibylla ad <u>ripam</u> (the river bank) <u>pedem advertunt</u> (turn their foot).

Iam Navita spectat eos advertere pedem ad ripam.

Ergo, primus, Navita eos <u>aggreditur dictis</u> (addresses with words) et <u>ultro increpat </u>(of his own accord shouts at [them]).

ORDO

Ergo peragunt iter inceptum,

-que propinquant fluvio:

quos ut navita iam inde ab Stygia unda prospexit ire per tacitum

nemus,

-que advertere pedem ripae,

sic prior aggreditur dictis, atque ultro increpat:

Carmen ipsum

Ergo iter inceptum peragunt fluvioque propinquant.

navita quos iam inde ut Stygia prospexit ab unda   385

per tacitum nemus ire pedemque advertere ripae,

sic prior adgreditur dictis atque increpat ultro:

Questions on *Aeneid* 6.384-387

1. What impression does this passage give of the geography of
the underworld?

2. How does Virgil emphasise Charon's quick temper?

388-397: Charon's speech about previous visits from mortals

Tier 1

"Quisquis (whoever) tu es,

qui venis ad nostrum fluvium cum armis,

dic mihi: cur huc venis?

et desiste ibi!

hic est locus mortuorum et somnis et noctis.

ego non possum portare homines viventes in mea rate.

ego tristis sum quia Hercules, Theseus et Pirithous venerunt huc,

quamquam filii deorum erant et nemo poterat superare eos.

Cerberus est canis.

Cerberus Tartarum custodit.

Hercules Cerberum sine armis ad terram cepit.

Hercules Cerberum ad terram portavit.

Theseus et Pirithous volebant capere uxorem Ditis (= Hades aut

Pluto).

ORDO

'Quisque es, qui tendis ad nostra flumina armatus,

age fare, quid venias,

et iam istinc comprime gressum.

Hic est locus umbrarum, somni -que soporae noctis:

nefas [est] vectare viva corpora Stygia carina.

Nec vero sum laetatus me lacu accespisse Alciden euntem,

nec Thesea, -que Pirithoum,

quanquam essent geniti dis atque invicti viribus.

Ille manu petivit Tartareum custodem in vincla,

-que traxit trementem solio regis ipsius;

hi adorti deducere dominam thalamo Ditis.'

Carmen ipsum

'quisquis es, armatus qui nostra ad flumina tendis,

fare age, quid venias, iam istinc et comprime gressum.

umbrarum hic locus est, somni noctisque soporae: 390

corpora viva nefas Stygia vectare carina.

nec vero Alciden me sum laetatus euntem

accepisse lacu, nec Thesea Pirithoumque,

dis quamquam geniti atque invicti viribus essent.

Tartareum ille manu custodem in vincla petivit   395

ipsius a solio regis traxitque trementem;

hi dominam Ditis thalamo deducere adorti.'

Questions on *Aeneid* 6.388-397

1. Research Hercules, Theseus and Pirithous: summarise each
   of their journeys into the underworld. In what ways are these
   men similar to and different from Aeneas?

Tier 1

Sibylla <u>breviter fata est</u> (briefly spoke):

'Sunt nullae <u>insidiae</u> (traps) hic

nec haec tela ferunt <u>vim</u> (violence):

Cerberus, ingens janitor, potest timere umbras mortuorum,

Proserpina, uxor Plutonis, potest servare domum Plutonis.

Pluto est deus mortuorum et frater Jovis.

Juppiter est pater Proserpinae,

ergo Pluto est patruus Proserpinae et maritus!

Trojanus Aeneas, notissimus pietate et armis,

ad patrem descendit.

Si Aeneas et eius magna pietas non movet te,

specta hunc <u>ramum</u> (branch)!

(Sibylla aureum ramum ex veste effert)

Ira Charontis abit.

ORDO

Contra quae Amphrysia vates breviter fata est:

'Nullae tales insidiae [sunt] hic (absiste moveri),

nec tela ferunt vim:

licet [ut] ingens janitor aeternum latrans [in] antro terreat exsanguis

umbras,

ut casta Proserpina sevet limen patrui.

Troius Aeneas, insignis pietate et armis,

descendit ad genitorem, ad imas umbras Erebi.

Si nulla imago tantae pietatis movet te,

at agnoscas hunc ramum

(aperit ramum qui latebat [sub] veste).

Tum corda residunt ex tumida ira;

Carmen ipsum

quae contra breviter fata est Amphrysia vates:

'nullae hic insidiae tales (absiste moveri),

nec vim tela ferunt; licet ingens ianitor antro   400

aeternum latrans exsanguis terreat umbras,

casta licet patrui servet Proserpina limen.

Troius Aeneas, pietate insignis et armis,

ad genitorem imas Erebi descendit ad umbras.

si te nulla movet tantae pietatis imago,   405

at ramum hunc' (aperit ramum qui veste latebat)

'agnoscas.' tumida ex ira tum corda residunt;

Questions on *Aeneid* 6.398-407

1. How is Proserpina (Persephone, in Greek) presented in line 402? How does the word order emphasise these qualities?

2. How is Aeneas described by the Sibyl?

3. In *Res Gestae* 34, Augustus states that the Senate and People of Rome (SPQR) gave him a golden shield to celebrate his virtues of *Virtus* (military might or bravery), *Clementia* (mercy), *Iustitia* (justice) and *Pietas* (piety or honour for Gods, family and state).

   Do you think Virgil is consciously drawing parallels between Aeneas and Augustus here? Why?

408-416: The Golden Bough

Tier 1

Sibylla non dicit plura verba quam haec verba.

Charon admirat antiquum donum <u>fatalis virgae</u> (fated staff)

Charon non viderat virgam diu,

Charon ad-vertit caeruleam (blue-green) ratem,

et approprinquat <u>ripae</u> (bank).

<u>inde</u> (there) Charon deturbat alias animas,

quae sedebant in longa linea,

et aperit <u>foros</u> (ship's gangway)

simul (at the same time) Charon accipit magnum Aenean

in cavo rate,

sutilis (stitched-together) et rimosa (cracked),

ratis gemit (groans) sub gravitate

et accipit multam paludem (swamp).

tandem Charon deposuit et vatem Sibyllam et virum Aenean

incolumnes (unharmed) trans fluvium in informi limo (mud)

et glauca (grey) ulva (reeds)

ORDO

nec plura his.

Ille admirans venerabile donum fatalis virgae,

visum post longo tempore, advertit caeruleam puppim,

-que propinquat ripae.

Inde deturbat alias animas, quae sedebant per longa iuga,

-que laxat foros; simul accipit ingentem Aenean [in] alveo.

Sutilis cymba gemuit sub pondere,

et rimosa accepit multam [aquam] paludem.

Tandem exponit -que vatem -que virum incolumes trans fluvium in

informi limo,

-que glauca ulva.

Carmen ipsum

nec plura his. ille admirans venerabile donum

fatalis virgae longo post tempore visum

caeruleam advertit puppim ripaeque propinquat.   410

inde alias animas, quae per iuga longa sedebant,

deturbat laxatque foros; simul accipit alveo

ingentem Aenean. gemuit sub pondere cumba

sutilis et multam accepit rimosa paludem.

tandem trans fluvium incolumis vatemque virumque   415

informi limo glaucaque exponit in ulua.

Questions on *Aeneid* 6.408-416

1. Why do you think Charon's boat struggles to carry Aeneas?

2. How does Virgil use language to emphasise the struggle?

3. Pick three adjectives from these lines and explain what they add to the passage.

Lines 679-712: Aeneas visits his father in Elysium

*Lines 679-686: While admiring his future descendants, Anchises
sees his son arriving.*

Tier 1

sed pater Anchises spectabat <u>animas</u> (souls).

animae erant <u>inclusae</u> (shut in)

<u>penitus</u> (deep within) <u>virenti</u> (green) valle.

Anchises spectabat animas et erat laetus.

animae ibant ad superum lumen.

forte Anchises numerabat omnes <u>suos</u> (his people)

et amatos <u>nepotes</u> (descendants)

et fata et fortunas virorum

et <u>mores</u> (customs) et <u>manus</u> (works)

et Anchises vidit Aenean, qui veniebat <u>adversus</u> (towards him) per

<u>gramina</u> (grass),

rapidus Anchises <u>tetendit</u> (held out) <u>utrasque</u> (both) palmas,

et lacrimavit,

et dixit,

ORDO

At pater Anchises lustrabat animas,

penitus inclusas virenti convalle,

-que ituras ad superum lumen, recolens studio,

-que forte recensebat omnem numerum suorum,

-que caros nepotes -que fata -que fortunas virorum

-que mores -que manus.

-que is, ubi vidit Aenean tendentem adversum per gramina,

alacris tetendit utrasque palmas,

-que lacrimae effusae genis, et vox excidit ore:

Carmen ipsum

At pater Anchises penitus convalle virenti

inclusas animas superumque ad lumen ituras   680

lustrabat studio recolens, omnemque suorum

forte recensebat numerum, carosque nepotes

fataque fortunasque virum moresque manusque.

isque ubi tendentem adversum per gramina vidit

Aenean, alacris palmas utrasque tetendit,   685

effusaeque genis lacrimae et vox excidit ore:

Questions on *Aeneid* 6.679-686

1. How does Virgil help us to imagine the reunion between Aeneas and Anchises?

2. What does Anchises admire about the souls he sees?

3. How does the landscape of this part of the underworld contrast with the banks of the river Styx?

Lines 687-694: Anchises speaks to Aeneas

Tier 1

[Anchises dicit] "venisti tandem?

et tua pietas vicit (has defeated) difficile iter (journey)?

ego sum tuus pater; ego scio te esse pium. igitur ego expectavi te.

mi fili, datur (is it given?) mihi spectare tuam faciem

et audire et respondere cum nota (known) voce?

sic (in this way) numerabam tempora et cogitabam

et putabam de futuro.

et mea cura non me fefellit (deceived).

accipio te portatum (carried) [per] quas terras!

et per quantas aquas!

accipio te iactatum (thrown about) quantis periculis, mi fili!

timui magnopere. timui regna Libyae.

timui ne regna Libyae nocerent (do harm) tibi.

ORDO

'venisti tandem?

-que tua pietas, exspectata parenti, vicit durum iter?

Nate, datur tueri tua ora,

et audire et reddere notas voces?

Sic equidem dinumerans tempora ducebam in animo,

-que rebar futurum;

nec mea cura fefellit me.

Accipio te vectum [per] quas terras,

et per quanta aequora,

[accipio te] iactatum quantis periculis, nate.

Quam metui, ne regna Libyae nocerent tibi [ali]quid.

Carmen ipsum

'venisti tandem, tuaque exspectata parenti

vicit iter durum pietas? datur ora tueri,

nate, tua et notas audire et reddere voces?

sic equidem ducebam animo rebarque futurum   690

tempora dinumerans, nec me mea cura fefellit.

quas ego te terras et quanta per aequora vectum

accipio! quantis iactatum, nate, periclis!

quam metui ne quid Libyae tibi regna nocerent!'

Questions on *Aeneid* 6.687-694:

1. How does Virgil emphasise Anchises' feelings of:

    a. fear,

    b. impatience and

    c. excitement?

Lines 695-702: They try to embrace

Tier 1

sed Aeneas (dixit):

"pater, tua <u>tristis</u> (sad) imago mihi venit saepe.

imago me iussit venire hic.

naves sunt in Tyrrheno mare.

pater, da mihi tuam <u>dextram</u> (right) <u>manum</u> (hand), da!

et noli fugere meum <u>amplexum</u> (hug)."

sic dicit,

simul (at the same time) lacrimabat magnopere.

ibi <u>ter</u> (three times)

<u>ter</u> (three times) non poterat amplecti (hug) patrem.

non poterat ponere bracchia (arms) circum collo (neck).

<u>ter</u> (three times) imago effugit manus (hands)

similis levibus (light) ventis (winds)

et simillima volucri (winged) somno (sleep)

ORDO

Autem ille (dixit):

'Genitor, tua, tua tristis imago,

occurrens saepius,

ad-egit me tendere haec limina.

Classes stant [in] Tyrrheno sale.

Genitor, da [mihi] iungere dextram, da;

-que ne subtrahe te nostro amplexu.'

Sic memorans,

simul rigabat ora largo fletu.

Ibi ter conatus dare bracchia circum collo;

ter imago frustra comprensa effugit manus,

par levibus ventis,

-que simillima volucri somno.

Carmen ipsum

ille autem: 'tua me, genitor, tua tristis imago   695

saepius occurrens haec limina tendere adegit;

stant sale Tyrrheno classes. da iungere dextram,

da, genitor, teque amplexu ne subtrahe nostro.'

sic memorans largo fletu simul ora rigabat.

ter conatus ibi collo dare bracchia circum;   700

ter frustra comprensa manus effugit imago,

par levibus ventis volucrique simillima somno.

Questions on *Aeneid* 6.695-702:

1. Why do you think sleep is often described as 'winged' ('volucri')?

2. Read the following scene from Homer's *Odyssey* (Book 11. 211-214):

"So she spoke, and I wondered how I might embrace my dead mother's ghost. Three times my will urged me to clasp her, and I started towards her, three times she escaped my arms like a shadow or a dream. And the pain seemed deeper in my heart." (A.S. Kline, 2004)

(N.B. Odysseus did not know his mother was dead when he saw her in the underworld)

In what ways does Virgil make his scene similar to Homer's and in what ways different? Why do you think he might have done this?

Lines 703-712: The River Lethe and the Bee simile

Tier 1

interea Aeneas videt nemus (grove) seclusa in

et arbores quae sonum faciunt

et fluvium Lethaeum, qui it per tranquillas villas .

multi populi volant circum

veluti (like) apes in agris consumunt multos flores in mensibus Iunio

et Iulio et Augusto

et turbae apium sunt circum alba lilia

sonus apium est murmur. murmur est magnus.

subito Aeneas est perterritus. Aeneas videt quidam.

Inscius Aeneas rogat:

Qui sunt illi fluvii?

Qui sunt illi viri in magna turba?

ORDO

Interea Aeneas videt seclusum nemus in reducta valle,

et virgulta sonantia silvae,

-que Lethaeum amnem,

qui praenatat [per] placidas domos.

Innumerae gentes -que populi volabant circum hunc:

ac veluti in pratis, uti apes insidunt variis floribus serena aestate,

et funduntur circum candida lilia,

omnis campus strepit murmure.

Aeneas horrescit subito visu,

-que inscius requirit causas,

quae sint porro ea flumina,

-ve qui viri compleverint ripas tanto agmine.

Carmen ipsum

Interea videt Aeneas in valle reducta

seclusum nemus et virgulta sonantia silvae,

Lethaeumque domos placidas qui praenatat amnem.   705

hunc circum innumerae gentes populique volabant:

ac veluti in pratis ubi apes aestate serena

floribus insidunt variis et candida circum

lilia funduntur, strepit omnis murmure campus.

horrescit visu subito causasque requirit   710

inscius Aeneas, quae sint ea flumina porro,

quive viri tanto complerint agmine ripas.

Questions on *Aeneid* 6.703-712:

1. Analyse the simile. What two things are being compared and what is the effect?

2. What is the 'mood' of the simile and how does it compare to the two similes at the river Styx in lines 309-316?

3. This is the second of three famous 'bee' similes in the *Aeneid*. They come in book 1, in book 12 (the final book) and here in book 6. What might this imply about the structure of the poem and the central importance of this moment of reunion between father and son?

Lines 752-759: Anchises unfolds the future of the Roman race

Tier 1

Anchises ducit filium Aenean et Sibyllam in mediam turbam

virorum.

Anchises tumulum (small hill) ascendit.

Unde (from where) posset spectare omnes viros

et discere facies virorum venientum in terram.

Anchises dicit:

"Nunc narrabo tibi gloriam

quae sequetur Troianam gentem.

Narrabo quoque de nepotibus tuis (your descendents)

qui ibunt in terram cum nomine nostro.

Et docebo te tua fata.

ORDO

Anchises dixerat

-que trahit natum -que Sibyllam una

in medios conventus -que sonantem turbam,

et capit tumulum,

unde posset legere omnes adversos [in] longo ordine,

et discere vultus venientum.

'Nunc, age, expediam dictis,

quae gloria deinde sequatur Dardaniam prolem,

qui nepotes maneant de Itala gente,

inlustris animas,

-que ituras in nostrum nomen,

et docebo te tua fata.'

Carmen ipsum

Dixerat Anchises natumque unaque Sibyllam

conventus trahit in medios turbamque sonantem,

et tumulum capit unde omnis longo ordine posset

adversos legere et venientum discere vultus.   755

'Nunc age, Dardaniam prolem quae deinde sequatur

gloria, qui maneant Itala de gente nepotes,

inlustris animas nostrumque in nomen ituras,

expediam dictis, et te tua fata docebo.

Questions on *Aeneid* 6.752-59:

1. How does Virgil's description of the crowd of souls in lines 752-755 compare to his description of the souls at the river Styx (lines 306-316)?

2. Who was Dardanus and why are the future Romans called Dardanian?

3. Research the role and purpose of *Initiation Ceremonies* in world history. To what extent does this scene and the whole set text qualify as an initiation ceremony or rite?

Lines 788-800: Augustus, the first Roman Emperor

Tier 1

Anchises, pater Aeneae, dicit:

Specta tuos populos,

tuos Romanos.

Hic est Julius Caesar

et hic sunt omnes liberi Iuli [Iulus est filius Aeneae].

Hi viri ad terram venient.

Hic est vir, quem saepe audis promitti tibi,

Augustus Caesar, filius divi,

qui feret bonas res ad Latium.

(Olim Saturnus, pater Jovis, regnabat Latium. Hoc tempus

nominatur 'aurea saecula').

Augustus feret imperium Romanum ad Africam et Indiam,

terrae quae iacent extra stellas,

ubi titanus Atlas caelum portat!

Iam nunc Caspia regna et Maeotia tellus [terra prope 'atrum mare']

et Aegyptus timent adventum Augusti.

ORDO

Huc flecte geminas acies [= oculos],

aspice hanc gentem -que tuos Romanos.

Hic [est] Caesar

et omnis [= omnes] progenies Iuli,

ventura sub magnum axem caeli.

Hic, hic est vir,

quem saepius audis promitti tibi,

Augustus Caesar,

genus divi,

qui rursus condet aurea secula Latio,

per arva [= agros] quondam regnata Saturno,

et proferet imperium super Garamantas et Indos;

tellus iacet extra sidera,

extra vias anni que solis,

ubi caelifer Atlas umero torquet axem aptum ardentibus stellis.

In adventum huius iam nunc et Caspia regna horrent responsis

divum,

et Maeotia tellus,

et trepida ostia septemgemini Nili turbant.

Carmen ipsum

huc geminas nunc flecte acies, hanc aspice gentem

Romanosque tuos. hic Caesar et omnis Iuli

progenies magnum caeli ventura sub axem.   790

hic vir, hic est, tibi quem promitti saepius audis,

Augustus Caesar, divi genus, aurea condet

saecula qui rursus Latio regnata per arva

Saturno quondam, super et Garamantas et Indos

proferet imperium; iacet extra sidera tellus,   795

extra anni solisque vias, ubi caelifer Atlas

axem umero torquet stellis ardentibus aptum.

huius in adventum iam nunc et Caspia regna

responsis horrent divum et Maeotia tellus,

et septemgemini turbant trepida ostia Nili.   800

Questions on *Aeneid* 6.788-800:

1. How does Virgil make Augustus (the Roman Emperor at the time he was writing) look impressive?

2. Why have OCR chosen to end their specification here? What message might they be proposing?

3. This passage is one of three direct references to the Emperor Augustus, along with Book 1.286-296 and Book 8.675-688 (given in translation below). Read all three passages and compare them. In what specific ways does Virgil praise Augustus?

Augustus in Book 1:

From this glorious source a Trojan Caesar will be born,

who will bound the empire with Ocean, his fame with the stars,

Augustus, a Julius, his name descended from the great Iulus.

You, no longer anxious, will receive him one day in heaven,

burdened with Eastern spoils: he'll be called to in prayer.

Then with wars abandoned, the harsh ages will grow mild:

White haired Trust, and Vesta, Quirinus with his brother Remus will make the laws: the gates of War, grim with iron,

and narrowed by bars, will be closed: inside impious Rage will roar

frighteningly from blood-stained mouth, seated on savage weapons,

hands tied behind his back, with a hundred knots of bronze.'

(A.S. Kline, 2004)

Augustus in Book 8:

On one side Augustus Caesar stands on the high stern,

leading the Italians to the conflict, with him the Senate,

the People, the household gods, the great gods, his happy brow

shoots out twin flames, and his father's star is shown on his head.

Elsewhere Agrippa, favoured by the winds and the gods

leads his towering column of ships, his brow shines

with the beaks of the naval crown, his proud battle distinction.

On the other side Antony, with barbarous wealth and strange weapons,

conqueror of eastern peoples and the Indian shores, bringing Egypt,

and the might of the Orient, with him, and furthest Bactria:

and his Egyptian consort follows him (the shame).

(A.S. Kline, 2002)

The Full GCSE set text

Now read the full text quickly (at the speed you would read English) as often as possible

295-316: Charon and the way to the underworld

Hinc via Tartarei quae fert Acherontis ad undas.   295

turbidus hic caeno vastaque voragine gurges

aestuat atque omnem Cocyto eructat harenam.

portitor has horrendus aquas et flumina servat

terribili squalore Charon, cui plurima mento

canities inculta iacet, stant lumina flamma,   300

sordidus ex umeris nodo dependet amictus.

ipse ratem conto subigit velisque ministrat

et ferruginea subvectat corpora cumba,

iam senior, sed cruda deo viridisque senectus.

huc omnis turba ad ripas effusa ruebat,   305

matres atque viri defunctaque corpora vita

magnanimum heroum, pueri innuptaeque puellae,

impositique rogis iuvenes ante ora parentum:

quam multa in silvis autumni frigore primo

lapsa cadunt folia, aut ad terram gurgite ab alto   310

quam multae glomerantur aves, ubi frigidus annus

trans pontum fugat et terris immittit apricis.

stabant orantes primi transmittere cursum

tendebantque manus ripae ulterioris amore.

navita sed tristis nunc hos nunc accipit illos,   315

ast alios longe summotos arcet harena.

384-416: The Golden Bough and crossing the Styx

Ergo iter inceptum peragunt fluvioque propinquant.

navita quos iam inde ut Stygia prospexit ab unda   385

per tacitum nemus ire pedemque advertere ripae,

sic prior adgreditur dictis atque increpat ultro:

'quisquis es, armatus qui nostra ad flumina tendis,

fare age, quid venias, iam istinc et comprime gressum.

umbrarum hic locus est, somni noctisque soporae: 390

corpora viva nefas Stygia vectare carina.

nec vero Alciden me sum laetatus euntem

accepisse lacu, nec Thesea Pirithoumque,

dis quamquam geniti atque invicti viribus essent.

Tartareum ille manu custodem in vincla petivit   395

ipsius a solio regis traxitque trementem;

hi dominam Ditis thalamo deducere adorti.'

quae contra breviter fata est Amphrysia vates:

'nullae hic insidiae tales (absiste moveri),

nec vim tela ferunt; licet ingens ianitor antro   400

aeternum latrans exsanguis terreat umbras,

casta licet patrui servet Proserpina limen.

Troius Aeneas, pietate insignis et armis,

ad genitorem imas Erebi descendit ad umbras.

si te nulla movet tantae pietatis imago,   405

at ramum hunc' (aperit ramum qui veste latebat)

'agnoscas.' tumida ex ira tum corda residunt;

nec plura his. ille admirans venerabile donum

fatalis virgae longo post tempore visum

caeruleam advertit puppim ripaeque propinquat.   410

inde alias animas, quae per iuga longa sedebant,

deturbat laxatque foros; simul accipit alveo

ingentem Aenean. gemuit sub pondere cumba

sutilis et multam accepit rimosa paludem.

tandem trans fluvium incolumis vatemque virumque   415

informi limo glaucaque exponit in ulua.

679-712: Aeneas visits his father in Elysium

At pater Anchises penitus convalle virenti

inclusas animas superumque ad lumen ituras   680

lustrabat studio recolens, omnemque suorum

forte recensebat numerum, carosque nepotes

fataque fortunasque virum moresque manusque.

isque ubi tendentem adversum per gramina vidit

Aenean, alacris palmas utrasque tetendit,   685

effusaeque genis lacrimae et vox excidit ore:

'venisti tandem, tuaque exspectata parenti

vicit iter durum pietas? datur ora tueri,

nate, tua et notas audire et reddere voces?

sic equidem ducebam animo rebarque futurum   690

tempora dinumerans, nec me mea cura fefellit.

quas ego te terras et quanta per aequora vectum

accipio! quantis iactatum, nate, periclis!

quam metui ne quid Libyae tibi regna nocerent!'

ille autem: 'tua me, genitor, tua tristis imago   695

saepius occurrens haec limina tendere adegit;

stant sale Tyrrheno classes. da iungere dextram,

da, genitor, teque amplexu ne subtrahe nostro.'

sic memorans largo fletu simul ora rigabat.

ter conatus ibi collo dare bracchia circum;   700

ter frustra comprensa manus effugit imago,

par levibus ventis volucrique simillima somno.

Interea videt Aeneas in valle reducta

seclusum nemus et virgulta sonantia silvae,

Lethaeumque domos placidas qui praenatat amnem.   705

hunc circum innumerae gentes populique volabant:

ac veluti in pratis ubi apes aestate serena

floribus insidunt variis et candida circum

lilia funduntur, strepit omnis murmure campus.

horrescit visu subito causasque requirit   710

inscius Aeneas, quae sint ea flumina porro,

quive viri tanto complerint agmine ripas.

752-759: Anchises unfolds the future of the Roman race

Dixerat Anchises natumque unaque Sibyllam

conventus trahit in medios turbamque sonantem,

et tumulum capit unde omnis longo ordine posset

adversos legere et venientum discere vultus.   755

'Nunc age, Dardaniam prolem quae deinde sequatur

gloria, qui maneant Itala de gente nepotes,

inlustris animas nostrumque in nomen ituras,

expediam dictis, et te tua fata docebo.

788-800: Augustus, the first Roman Emperor

huc geminas nunc flecte acies, hanc aspice gentem

Romanosque tuos. hic Caesar et omnis Iuli

progenies magnum caeli ventura sub axem.   790

hic vir, hic est, tibi quem promitti saepius audis,

Augustus Caesar, divi genus, aurea condet

saecula qui rursus Latio regnata per arva

Saturno quondam, super et Garamantas et Indos

proferet imperium; iacet extra sidera tellus,   795

extra anni solisque vias, ubi caelifer Atlas

axem umero torquet stellis ardentibus aptum.

huius in adventum iam nunc et Caspia regna

responsis horrent divum et Maeotia tellus,

et septemgemini turbant trepida ostia Nili.

Glossary

This glossary was made using Collatinus 11.2.
Collatinus 11.2 is a free and open tool developed by Yves Ouvrard and Philippe Verkerk, which can be downloaded from https://outils.biblissima.fr/en/collatinus/.

ab
ā, ăb, ābs, prép. + abl. (5874) : by (agent), from (departure, cause, remote origin/time);
absiste
ābsīsto, is, ere, stiti, - (22) : to withdraw from; to desist, cease; to leave off; to depart, go away from; to stand back;
ac
āc, conj. coord. (5185) : and, and also, and besides;
accepisse
āccĭpĭo, is, ere, cepi, ceptum (1826) : to take, grasp, receive, accept, undertake; to admit, let in, hear, learn; to obey;
accepit
āccĭpĭo, is, ere, cepi, ceptum (1826) : to take, grasp, receive, accept, undertake; to admit, let in, hear, learn; to obey;
accipio
āccĭpĭo, is, ere, cepi, ceptum (1826) : to take, grasp, receive, accept, undertake; to admit, let in, hear, learn; to obey;
accipit
āccĭpĭo, is, ere, cepi, ceptum (1826) : to take, grasp, receive, accept, undertake; to admit, let in, hear, learn; to obey;
acherontis
Ăchĕrōn, ontis, m. (20) : Acheron, the stream of woe
acies
ăcĭēs, ei, f. (654) : sharpness, sharp edge, point; battle line/array; sight, glance; pupil of eye;
ad
ăd, prép. + acc. (11922) : to, up to, towards; near, at; until, on, by; almost; according to; about w/NUM;
adegit
ădīgo, is, ere, egi, actum (84) : to drive in/to (cattle), force, impel; to cast, hurl; to consign (curse); to bind (oath);
adgreditur
ādgrĕdĭŏr, eris, i, gressus sum (162) : aller vers, s'approcher, aborder, attaquer
āggrĕdĭo, ĕre : act., to go to, approach, adgreditur, adgreditor, Pass.
admirans
ādmīrŏr, aris, ari, atus sum (95) : to wonder at, to be astonished at, to regard with admiration, to admire
adorti
ădŏrĭŏr, iris, iri, adortus sum (63) : to rise up for the purpose of going to some one, something, of undertaking something great, difficult, hazardous
adventum
ādvēntus, us, m. (301) : arrival, approach; visit, appearance, advent; ripening; invasion, incursion;

ādvĕnĭo, is, ire, ueni, uentum (178) : to come to, to arrive; to arrive at, to reach, be brought; to develop, set in, to arise;

adversos

ādvērsus, a, um (326) : facing, opposite, against, towards; contrary to; face to face, in presence of;

ādvērto, (aduorto) is, ere, uerti, uersum (96) : to turn/face to/towards; to direct/draw one's attention to; to steer/pilot (ship);

adversum

ādvērsus, a, um (326) : facing, opposite, against, towards; contrary to; face to face, in presence of;

ādvērto, (aduorto) is, ere, uerti, uersum (96) : to turn/face to/towards; to direct/draw one's attention to; to steer/pilot (ship);

ādvērsŭm, cf. adversus2 (4) : renvoi non trouvé

advertere

ādvērto, (aduorto) is, ere, uerti, uersum (96) : to turn/face to/towards; to direct/draw one's attention to; to steer/pilot (ship);

advertit

ādvērto, (aduorto) is, ere, uerti, uersum (96) : to turn/face to/towards; to direct/draw one's attention to; to steer/pilot (ship);

aenean

Āenēās, ae, m. (292) : Aeneas

aeneas

āenĕus, a, um (24) : copper, of copper (alloy); bronze, made of bronze, bronze-colored; brazen;

aequora

āequŏr, oris, n. (281) : level/smooth surface, plain; surface of the sea; sea, ocean;

aestate

āestās, tatis, f. (139) : summer; summer heat/weather; a year;

aestuat

āestŭo, as, are (41) : to boil, seethe, foam; to billow roll in waves; to be agitated/hot; to burn; to waver;

aeternum

āetērnus, a, um (232) : eternal/everlasting/imperishable; perpetual, w/out start/end; [in ~=>forever];

āetērnŭm, adv. (14) : forever

age

ăgĕ, interj. (168) : come!, go to!, well!, all right!; let come;

ăgo, is, ere, egi, actum (2556) : to drive/urge/conduct/act; to spend (time w/cum); to thank (w/gratias); deliver

agmine

āgmĕn, inis, n. (521) : stream; herd, flock, troop, crowd; marching army, column, line; procession;

agnoscas

āgnōsco, is, ere, noui, nitum (167) : to recognize, realize, discern; to acknowledge, claim, admit to/responsibility;

alacris

ălăcĕr, cris, cre (59) : eager/keen/spirited; quick/brisk; active/lively; courageous/ready; cheerful;

ălăcris, ĭs, ĕ cf. alacer (4) : eager/keen/spirited; quick/brisk; active/lively; courageous/ready; cheerful;

alciden
Ālcīdēs, ae, m. (121) : a male descendant of Alceus;, his grandson Hercules

alias
ălĭus, a, ud, pron. (4524) : the_one ... the_other (alius ... alius);
ălĭās, adv. (97) : at/in another time/place; previously, subsequently; elsewhere; otherwise;

alios
ălĭus, a, ud, pron. (4524) : the_one ... the_other (alius ... alius);

alto
ăltus, a, um (719) : high; deep/profound; shrill; lofty/noble; deep rooted; far-fetched; grown
ăltŭm, i, n. (158) : deeply, deep; high, on high, from above;
ălo, is, ere, ui, altum (alitum) (224) : to feed, nourish, rear, nurse, suckle; to cherish; to support, maintain, develop;

alveo
ālvĕus, i, m. (64) : - cavity, hollow; tub; trough, bowl, tray; gameboard; beehive; canoe; - hold (ship), ship, boat; channel, bed (river), trench;

amictus
ămīctus, us, m. (50) : cloak, mantle; outer garment; clothing, garb; fashion; manner of dress;
ămīcĭo, is, ire, icui et ixi, ictum (21) : clothe, cover, dress; wrap about; surround; veil; clothe with words;

amnem
āmnĭs, is, m. (337) : river (real/personified), stream; current; (running) water; the river Ocean;

amore
ămŏr, oris, m. (1105) : love; affection; the beloved; Cupid; affair; sexual/illicit/homosexual passion;

amphrysia
Āmphrȳsĭus, a, um (2) : belonging to Amphrysus, to Apollo

amplexu
āmplĕxus, us, m. (66) : clasp, embrace, surrounding; sexual embrace; coil (snake); circumference;
āmplĕctŏr, eris, i, amplexus sum (107) : to wind or twine round a person or thing (aliquem, πλέκεσθαι ἀμφίτινα, v. adimo), to surround, encompass, encircle

anchises
Ānchīsēs, ae, m., npr. (55) : Son of Capys, father of Æneas, who bore him forth from burning Troy upon his shoulders

animas
ănĭma, ae, f. (351) : soul, spirit, vital principle; life; breathing; wind, breeze; air (element);
ănĭmo, as, are (3) : to animate, give/bring life; to revive, refresh; to rouse, animate; to inspire; to blow;

animo
ănĭmus, i, m. (4155) : mind; intellect; soul; feelings; heart; spirit, courage, character, pride; air;
ănĭmo, as, are (3) : to animate, give/bring life; to revive, refresh; to rouse, animate; to inspire; to blow;

anni

ānnus, i, m. (1333) : year (astronomical/civil); age, time of life; year's produce; circuit, course;

annus

ānnus, i, m. (1333) : year (astronomical/civil); age, time of life; year's produce; circuit, course;

ante

āntĕ, prép. +acc. (942) : in front/presence of, in view; before (space/time/degree); over against,

āntēs, ium, m. (3) : rows, ranks

antro

āntrŭm, i, n. (91) : cave; cavern; hollow place with overarching foliage; cavity, hollow; tomb;

aperit

ăpĕrĭo, is, ire, ui, apertum (258) : to uncover, open, disclose; to explain, recount; to reveal; to found; to excavate; to spread out;

apes

ăpĭs, is, f. (52) : bee; swarm regarded as a portent; Apis, sacred bull worshiped in Egypt;

apricis

ăprīcus, a, um (16) : sunny, having lots of sunshine; warmed by/exposed to/open to the sun, basking;

ăprīcum, i, n. (2) : sunny place

aptum

āptus, a, um (259) : suitable, adapted; ready; apt, proper; tied, attached to; dependent on (w/ex);

ăpīscŏr, eris, i, aptus sum (11) : to reach after, in order to take, seize, get possession of

aquas

ăqua, ae, f. (915) : water; sea, lake; river, stream; rain, rainfall (pl.), rainwater; spa; urine;

arcet

ārcĕo, es, ere, ui (98) : to ward/keep off/away; to keep close, confine; to prevent, hinder; to protect; to separate;

ardentibus

ārdĕo, es, ere, arsi, arsurus (236) : to be on fire; to burn, blaze; to flash; to glow, sparkle; to rage; to be in a turmoil/love;

ārdēns, entis (95) : glowing, fiery, hot, ablaze, sparkling, gleaming, fiery, Burning, ardent, impassioned

armatus

ārmātus, a, um (265) : armed, equipped; defensively armed, armor clad; fortified; of the use of arms;

ārmo, as, are (143) : to equip, fit with armor; to arm; to strengthen; to rouse, stir; to incite war; to rig (ship);

ārmātŭs, us, m. (3) : armor, armed soldiers

armis

ārma, orum, n. pl. (1773) : Implements of war, arms, both of defence and offence

ārmus, i, m. (14) : inct., the shoulder where it is fitted to the shoulder-blade, the fore quarter, the shoulder of an animal, umerus

arva

ārvŭm, i, n. (198) : female external genitalia (rude);

aspice

āspǐcǐo, is, ere, spexi, spectum (429) : to look/gaze on/at, see, observe, behold, regard; to face; to consider, contemplate;
ast
āst, conj. (36) : but, on the other hand/contrary; but yet; at least; in that event; if further;
at
ǎt, conj. coord. (2174) : but, but on the other hand; on the contrary; while, whereas; but yet; at least;
atlas
Ātlās, antis, m. (13) : Atlas, a high mountain in Mauretania, in the northwest part of Libya, on which, heaven rested
atque
ātquĕ, conj. coord. (6931) : and, as well/soon as; together with; and moreover/even; and too/also/now; yet;
audire
āudǐo, is, ire, iui, itum (1713) : to hear, listen, accept, agree with; to obey; to harken, pay attention; to be able to hear;
audis
āudǐo, is, ire, iui, itum (1713) : to hear, listen, accept, agree with; to obey; to harken, pay attention; to be able to hear;
augustus
āugūstus, a, um (19) : sacred, venerable; majestic, august, solemn; dignified; worthy of honor (Ecc); The Emperor Augustus.
aurea
āurĕus, a, um (265) : of gold, golden; gilded; gold bearing; gleaming like gold; beautiful, splendid;
aut
āut, conj. coord. (6784) : or, or rather/else; either...or (aut...aut) (emphasizing one);
autem
āutĕm, conj. coord. (2095) : but (postpositive), on the other hand/contrary; while, however; moreover, also;
autumni
āutūmnus, i, m. (47) : of autumn, autumnal;
āutūmnus, a, um (2) : autumnal; subst. m. The season of abundance, the autumn
aves
ǎvǐs, is, f. (194) : bird; sign, omen, portent;
axem
āxǐs, is, m. (56) : - axle, axis, pole; chariot; the sky, heaven; north pole; region, clime; - Indian quadruped; (spotted deer?); - plank, board;
bracchia
brācchǐum, ii, n. (122) : arm; lower arm, forearm; claw; branch, shoot; earthwork connecting forts;
breviter
brĕvǐtĕr, adv. (75) : shortly, briefly, in a nut shell; quickly; for/within a short distance/time;
cadunt
cǎdo, is, ere, cecidi, casum (687) : to fall, sink, drop, plummet, topple; to be slain, die; to end, cease, abate; to decay;
caeli

cāelŭm, cōelum, i, n. (940) : - chisel; engraving tool; burin; - heaven, sky, heavens; space; air, climate, weather; universe, world; Jehovah;

caelifer
cāelĭfĕr, era, erum (4) : supporting the heavens

caeno
cāenŭm, i, n. (30) : mud, mire, filth, slime, dirt, uncleanness; (of persons) scum/filth;
cāeno, as, are : to dine, eat dinner/supper; to have dinner with; to dine on, make a meal of;

caeruleam
cāerŭlĕus, a, um (55) : blue, cerulean, dark; greenish-blue, azure; of river/sea deities; of sky/sea;

caesar
cāesăr, ăris, m. : c. caeso

campus
cāmpus, i, m. (456) : plain; level field/surface; open space for battle/games; sea; scope; campus;

candida
cāndĭdus, a, um (187) : - bright, clear, transparent; clean/spotless; lucid; candid; kind; innocent, pure; - radiant, unclouded; (dressed in) white; of light color; fair skinned, pale;

canities
cānĭtĭes, ei, f. (21) : white/gray coloring/deposit; gray/white hair, grayness of hair; old age;

capit
căpĭo, is, ere, cepi, captum (1382) : taking/seizing; [usus ~ => getting ownership by continued possession];

carina
cărīna, ae, f. (85) : keel, bottom of ship, hull; boat, ship, vessel; voyage; half walnut shell;

carosque
cārus, chārus, a, um (406) : dear, beloved; costly, precious, valued; high-priced, expensive;

caspia
Cāspĭus, a, um (14) : of or belonging to the Caspian Sea, Caspian; subst. m. sc. mons; subst. f. pl. sc. portae

casta
cāstus, a, um (153) : pure, moral; chaste, virtuous, pious; sacred; spotless; free from/untouched by;

causasque
cāusa, cāussa, ae, f. (3408) : for sake/purpose of (preceded by GEN.), on account/behalf of, with a view to;

charon
Chărōn, ontis, m. : Charon, a ferryman in the Lower World

circum
cīrcŭm, adv. (108) : around, about, among, near (space/time), in neighborhood of; in circle around;
cīrcus, i, m. (52) : race course; circus in Rome, celebration of games; circle; orbit;

classes
clāssĭs, is, f. (498) : class/division of Romans; grade (pupils); levy/draft; fleet/navy; group/band;

cocyto
Cōcȳtŏs, i, m. (15) : a mythic river in the Lower World
Cōcȳtus, i, m. : a mythic river in the Lower World

collo
cōllŭm, i, n. (244) : neck; throat; head and neck; severed head; upper stem (flower); mountain ridge;
cōllus, i, m. cf. collum (5) : neck; throat; head and neck; severed head; upper stem (flower); mountain ridge;
complerint
cōmplĕo, es, ere, pleui, pletum (167) : - to fill (up/in); to be big enough to fill; to occupy space, crowd; to furnish/supply/man; to satisfy;
comprensa
cōmprĕhēndo, cōmprēndo, is, ere, prehendi, prehensum (79) : - to catch/seize/grasp firmly; to arrest; to take hold/root/fire, ignite; to conceive - to embrace; to include/cover/deal with (in speech/law); to express (by term/symbol);
comprime
cōmprĭmo, is, ere, pressi, pressum (101) : - to press/squeeze together, fold, crush; to hem/shut/keep/hold in; to copulate (male);
conatus
cōnŏr, aris, ari (238) : to undertake, endeavor, attempt, try, venture, presume
cōnātus, us, m. (70) : attempt, effort; exertion, struggle; impulse, tendency; endeavor, design;
condet
cōndo, is, ere, didi, ditum (335) : to put/insert (into); to store up/put away, preserve, bottle (wine); to bury/inter; - to build/found, make; to shut (eyes); to conceal/hide/keep safe; to put together, - to restore; sheathe (sword); to plunge/bury (weapon in enemy); to put out of sight;
conto
cōntus, i, m. (17) : long pole esp. used on ship); lance, pike;
convalle
cōnvāllĭs, is, f. (21) : valley (much shut in), ravine, deep/narrow/enclosed valley, glen; (also pl.);
conventus
cōnvĕnĭo, is, ire, ueni, uentum (515) : it agrees/came together/is agreed/asserted; [bene ~ nobis=>we're on good
cōnvēntus, us, m. (117) : convent, monastery; religious community; convention (Ecc);
corda
cŏr, cordis, n. (192) : heart; mind/soul/spirit; intellect/judgment; sweetheart; souls/persons (pl.);
chōrda, cōrda, ae, f. (23) : tripe; catgut, musical instrument (string); rope/cord (binding slave) (L+S);
cōrdus, a, um (2) : lateborn, produced late in the season, the second crop of hay, after-math
corpora
cōrpŭs, oris, n. (2313) : - body; person, self; virility; flesh; corpse; trunk; frame(work); collection/ - substantial/material/concrete object/body; particle/atom; corporation, guild;
cruda
crūdus, a, um (47) : - raw; bloody/bleeding; crude, cruel, rough, merciless; fierce/savage; - youthful/hardy/vigorous; fresh/green/immature; undigested; w/undigested food;
cui
quī, quae, quod, pron. rel. (41601) : who; that; which, what; of which kind/degree; person/thing/time/point that
quĭs, quae, quid, pron. interr. (13642) : who? which? what? what man?

cumba

cūmba, ae, f. (27) : skiff, small boat; (esp. that in which Charon ferried the dead)

cura

cūra, ae, f. (932) : - concern, worry, anxiety, trouble; attention, care, pains, zeal; cure, - office/task/responsibility/post; administration, supervision; command (army);

cūro, cŏiro, as, are (419) : to arrange/see/attend to; to take care of; to provide for; to worry/care about; to heal/ - to undertake; to procure; to regard w/anxiety/interest; to take trouble/interest; to desire;

cursum

cūrsus, us, m. (437) : lesson;

cūrro, is, ere, cucurri, cursum (237) : to run/trot/gallop, hurry/hasten/speed, move/travel/proceed/flow swiftly/quickly;

custodem

cūstōs, odis, m. (312) : - guard; sentry/watch; guardian/protector/keeper; doorkeeper/watchman/janitor; shoot;

da

dŏ, das, dare, dedi, datum (5043) : - to give; dedicate; to sell; to pay; to grant/bestow/impart/offer/lend; to devote; to allow; - to surrender/give over; to send to die; to ascribe/attribute; to give birth/produce;

dardaniam

Dārdănĭus, a, um (50) : dardanian

Dārdănĭa, ae, f. (8) : the city Dardania, in Troas

dare

dŏ, das, dare, dedi, datum (5043) : - to give; dedicate; to sell; to pay; to grant/bestow/impart/offer/lend; to devote; to allow; - to surrender/give over; to send to die; to ascribe/attribute; to give birth/produce;

datur

dŏ, das, dare, dedi, datum (5043) : - to give; dedicate; to sell; to pay; to grant/bestow/impart/offer/lend; to devote; to allow; - to surrender/give over; to send to die; to ascribe/attribute; to give birth/produce;

deducere

dēdūco, is, ere, duxi, ductum (356) : - to lead/draw//pull/bring/stretch down/away/out/off; to escort; to eject/evict - to divert/draw (water); to draw (sword); to spin; to deduct/reduce/lessen; to describe; - to launch/bring downstream (ship); to remove (force); to entice; to found/settle

defunctaque

dēfūngŏr, eris, i, functus sum (65) : to settle a case (for so much); to make do; to discharge; to die; (PERF) to have died

deinde

deīndĕ, deīn, adv. (1200) : then/next/afterward; thereon/henceforth/from there/then; in next position/

deo

dĕus, i, m. (2679) : a god, a deity

dependet

dēpēndĕo, es, ere (24) : to hang on/from/down (from); to depend; to depend upon/on; to proceed/be derived from;

dēpēndo, is, ere, pendi, pensum (11) : Act., to pay

descendit

dēscēndo, is, ere, di, sum (227) : to descend, climb/march/come/go/flow/run/hang down; to dismount; to penetrate/sink;
deturbat
dētūrbo, as, are (27) : to upset/topple, bring tumbling down; to dislodge; to strike/beat to ground;
dextram
dēxtră, dēxtĕra, ou dextera, ae, f. (283) : on the right of; on the right-hand side of;
dēxtĕr, tra, trum (156) : right, on/to the right hand/side; skillful/dexterous/handy;
dictis
dīco, is, ere, dixi, dictum (7210) : to say, declare, state; to allege, declare positively; to assert; to plead (case); to mean;
dīctŭm, i, n. (352) : words/utterance/remark; one's word/promise; saying/maxim; bon mot, witticism;
dinumerans
dīnŭmĕro, as, are (8) : to count over, reckon up, enumerate
dis
dĕus, i, m. (2679) : a god, a deity
dīus, a, um (9) : of or belonging to a deity, divine.
dīs, dītis (2) : rich
discere
dīsco, is, ere, didici (441) : to learn; to hear, get to know, become acquainted with; to acquire knowledge/skill of/
ditis
dīvĭtĭāe, dītĭāe, arum, f. pl. (274) : wealth
dīvĕs, itis (311) : rich/wealthy; costly; fertile/productive (land); talented, well endowed;
dīs, dītis (2) : rich
divi
dīvus, i, m. (84) : divine; blessed, saint (Latham);
dīvus, a, um (137) : divine; blessed, saint (Latham);
dīvum, i, n. (6) : the sky, under the open sky, in the open air;
divum
dĕus, i, m. (2679) : a god, a deity
dīvus, i, m. (84) : divine; blessed, saint (Latham);
dīvus, a, um (137) : divine; blessed, saint (Latham);
dīvum, i, n. (6) : the sky, under the open sky, in the open air;
dixerat
dīco, is, ere, dixi, dictum (7210) : to say, declare, state; to allege, declare positively; to assert; to plead (case); to mean;
docebo
dŏcĕo, es, ere, cui, ctum (597) : to teach, show, point out;
dominam
dŏmĭna, ae, f. (233) : mistress of a family, wife; lady, lady-love; owner;
domos
dŏmus, us ou i, f. (2011) : house, building; home, household; (N 4 1, older N 2 1); [domu => at home];
donum
dŏnŭm, i, n. (316) : gift, present; offering;
ducebam

dūco, is, ere, duxi, ductum (1071) : to lead, command; to think, consider, regard; to prolong; durum

dūrus, a, um (541) : hard, stern; harsh, rough, vigorous; cruel, unfeeling, inflexible; durable;

ea

īs, ea, id, adj. et pron. (18209) : he/she/it/they (by GENDER/NUMBER); DEMONST that, he/she/it, they/them;

ĕā, adv. (11) : par cet endroit

effugit

ēffŭgĭo, is, ere, fugi, fugiturus (226) : to flee/escape; to run/slip/keep away (from), eschew/avoid; to baffle, escape notice;

effusa

ēffŭndo, is, ere, fudi, fusum (241) : - to pour out/away/off; to allow to drain; to shower; to volley (missiles); to send/stream - to shed (blood/tears); to discharge (vomit/urine), debouch, emit; to flow out, - to break out; to bear/yield/bring forth; to expend/use up; to unseat, eject/drop/discard;

ēffŭsus, a, um (36) : vaste, large, libre

effusaeque

ēffŭndo, is, ere, fudi, fusum (241) : - to pour out/away/off; to allow to drain; to shower; to volley (missiles); to send/stream - to shed (blood/tears); to discharge (vomit/urine), debouch, emit; to flow out, - to break out; to bear/yield/bring forth; to expend/use up; to unseat, eject/drop/discard;

ēffŭsus, a, um (36) : vaste, large, libre

ego

ĕgŏ̆, mei, pron. (14846) : moi, me

equidem

ĕquīdĕm, adv. (273) : truly, indeed; for my part;

erebi

Ĕrĕbus, i, m. (20) : The god of darkness, son of Chaos, and brother of Nox

ergo

ērgō, conj. (1450) : therefore; well, then, now;

eructat

ērūcto, as, are (7) : to bring up noisily; to discharge violently;

essent

sŭm, es, esse, fui (40916) : to be; to exist; (also used to form verb perfect passive tenses) with NOM PERF PPL

ĕdo, edis, esse, edi, esum (99) : to eat/consume/devour; to eat away (fire/water/disease); to destroy; to spend money on

est

sŭm, es, esse, fui (40916) : to be; to exist; (also used to form verb perfect passive tenses) with NOM PERF PPL

ĕdo, edis, esse, edi, esum (99) : to eat/consume/devour; to eat away (fire/water/disease); to destroy; to spend money on

euntem

ĕo, is, ire, iui, itum (1447) : to go (of every kind of motion of animate or inanimate things), to walk, ride, sail, fly, move, pass;

ex

ēx, prép. + abl. (6934) : out of, from; by reason of; according to; because of, as a result of;

excidit

ēxcīdo, is, ere, cidi (118) : to perish; to disappear; to escape, fall out; to be deprived of; to lose control of senses;

ēxcīdo, is, ere, cidi, cisum (43) : enlever en taillant, creuser

ēxcīndo, is, ere, cidi, cissum (28) : to demolish/destroy, raze to ground (town/building); to exterminate/destroy (people);

expediam

ēxpĕdĭo, is, ire, i(u)i , itum (221) : to disengage, loose, set free; to be expedient; to procure, obtain, make ready;

exponit

ēxpōno, is, ere, posui, positum (199) : to set/put forth/out; to abandon, expose; to publish; to explain, relate; to disembark;

exsanguis

ēxsānguĭs, e (41) : bloodless, pale, wan, feeble; frightened;

exspectata

ēxspēcto, as, are, aui, atum (404) : to lookout for, await; to expect, anticipate, hope for;

ēxpēctātus, a, um (2) : attendu

extra

ēxtrā, prép. + acc. (265) : outside of, beyond, without, beside; except;

fare

fŏr, aris, fari, fatus sum (103) : to speak, say

fata

fātŭm, i, n. (608) : utterance, oracle; fate, destiny; natural term of life; doom, death, calamity;

fŏr, aris, fari, fatus sum (103) : to speak, say

fatalis

fātālĭs, e (63) : fated, destined; fatal, deadly;

fataque

fātŭm, i, n. (608) : utterance, oracle; fate, destiny; natural term of life; doom, death, calamity;

fŏr, aris, fari, fatus sum (103) : to speak, say

fefellit

fāllo, is, ere, fĕfēlli, fālsum (fāllītum) (453) : to deceive; to slip by; to disappoint; to be mistaken, beguile, drive away; to fail; cto heat;

ferruginea

fērrūgĭnĕus, a, um (3) : of the color of iron-rust, somber;

fert

fĕro, fers, ferre, tuli, latum (3111) : to bring, bear; to tell/speak of; to consider; to carry off, win, receive, produce; to get;

ferunt

fĕro, fers, ferre, tuli, latum (3111) : to bring, bear; to tell/speak of; to consider; to carry off, win, receive, produce; to get;

flamma

flāmma, ae, f. (461) : flame, blaze; ardor, fire of love; object of love;

flāmmo, as, are (14) : to inflame, set on fire; to excite;

flecte

flēcto, is, ere, flexi, flexum (226) : to bend, curve, bow; to turn, curl; to persuade, prevail on, soften;

fletu

flētus, us, m. (117) : weeping, crying, tears; wailing; lamenting;

flĕo, es, ere, fleui, fletum (324) : to cry for; to cry, weep;

floribus

flōs, oris, m. (182) : flower, blossom; youthful prime;

flumina

flūměn, inis, n. (658) : river, stream; any flowing fluid; flood; onrush; [adverso ~ => against

fluvioque

flŭvĭus, i, m. (79) : river, stream; running water;

fluvium

flŭvĭus, i, m. (79) : river, stream; running water;

folia

fŏlĭŭm, ii, n. (82) : leaf;

foros

fŏrus, i, m. : gangway in a ship; row of benches erected for games/circus; cell of bees;

forte

fōrtĕ, adv. (566) : by chance; perhaps, perchance; as luck would have it;

fōrtĭs, e (884) : strong, powerful, mighty, vigorous, firm, steadfast, courageous, brave, bold;

fōrs, fortis, f. (60) : chance, hap, luck, hazard. Fors

fortunasque

fōrtūna, ae, f. (1523) : chance, luck, fate; prosperity; condition, wealth, property;

fōrtūno, as, are (3) : to make prosperous, fortunate, to make happy, to prosper, bless

frigidus

frīgĭdus, a, um (162) : cold, cool, chilly, frigid; lifeless, indifferent, dull;

frigore

frīgŭs, oris, n. (184) : cold; cold weather, winter; frost;

frīgŏr, oris, m. : cold; chill (esp. of feverish person) (Souter);

frustra

frūstrā, adv. (253) : in vain; for nothing, to no purpose;

frūstro, as, are (4) : to reject; delay; to rob/defraud/cheat; to pretend; to refute (argument); to corrupt/falsify;

fugat

fŭgo, as, are (90) : to put to flight, rout; to chase away; to drive into exile;

funduntur

fūndo, is, ere, fusi, fusum (263) : to pour, pour out, shed;

futurum

sŭm, es, esse, fui (40916) : to be; to exist; (also used to form verb perfect passive tenses) with NOM PERF PPL

fŭtūrus, a, um, part. fut. de sum (98) : about to be; future;

geminas

gĕmĭnus, a, um (163) : twin, double; twin-born; both;

gĕmĭno, as, are (15) : to double; to repeat; to double the force of; to pair (with);

gemuit

gĕmo, is, ere, gemui, gemitum (128) : to moan, groan; to lament (over); to grieve that; to give out a hollow sound (music, hit);

genis

gīgno, gĕno, is, ere, genui, genitum (253) : to give birth to, bring forth, bear; to beget; to be born (PASSIVE);

gĕna, ae, f. (104) : cheeks (pl.); eyes;

gĕnĭus, ii, m. (31) : genius;

geniti

gīgno, gĕno, is, ere, genui, genitum (253) : to give birth to, bring forth, bear; to beget; to be born (PASSIVE);

genitor

gĕnītŏr, oris, m. (148) : father; creator; originator;

gīgno, gĕno, is, ere, genui, genitum (253) : to give birth to, bring forth, bear; to beget; to be born (PASSIVE);

genitorem

gĕnītŏr, oris, m. (148) : father; creator; originator;

gente

gēns, gentis, f. (911) : tribe, clan; nation, people; Gentiles;

gentem

gēns, gentis, f. (911) : tribe, clan; nation, people; Gentiles;

gentes

gēns, gentis, f. (911) : tribe, clan; nation, people; Gentiles;

genus

gĕnŭs, eris, n. (1488) : - birth/descent/origin; race/family/house/stock/ancestry; offspring/descent;

gĕnŭ, us, n. (111) : knee;

glaucaque

glāucus, a, um (10) : bright, sparkling, gleaming, grayish

glomerantur

glŏmĕro, as, are (24) : to wind, form into a ball, gather into a round heap, to conglobate,

gloria

glōrĭa, ae, f. (798) : glory, fame; ambition; renown; vainglory, boasting;

gramina

grāmĕn, inis, n. (65) : grass, turf; herb; plant;

gressum

grēssus, us, m. (51) : going; step; the feet (pl.);

grădĭŏr, eris, i, gressus sum, intr. (27) : to take steps, to step, walk, go

gurges

gūrgēs, itis, m. (80) : "whirlpool; raging abyss; gulf, the sea; ""flood"", ""stream"";"

gurgite

gūrgēs, itis, m. (80) : "whirlpool; raging abyss; gulf, the sea; ""flood"", ""stream"";"

haec

hīc, haec, hoc, adj. pron. (20391) : this; these

hanc

hīc, haec, hoc, adj. pron. (20391) : this; these

harena

hărēna, ae, f. (139) : sand, grains of sand; sandy land or desert; seashore; arena, place of contest;

harenam

hărēna, ae, f. (139) : sand, grains of sand; sandy land or desert; seashore; arena, place of contest;

heroum

hērōs, herois, m. (50) : hero; demigod; (only sing.);

hērōus, a, um (5) : I. of or relating to a hero, heroic. Subst. m. an epic verse. II. Herous

hic

hīc, haec, hoc, adj. pron. (20391) : this; these

71

hīc, adv. (974) : here, in this place; in the present circumstances;

hinc

hīnc, adv. (852) : from here, from this source/cause; hence, henceforth;

his

hīc, haec, hoc, adj. pron. (20391) : this; these

horrendus

hŏrrĕo, es, ere, horrui, - (110) : to dread, shrink from, shudder at; to stand on end, bristle; to have rough appearance;

hŏrrēndus, a, um (50) : horrible, dreadful, terrible;

horrent

hŏrrĕo, es, ere, horrui, - (110) : to dread, shrink from, shudder at; to stand on end, bristle; to have rough appearance;

horrescit

hŏrrēsco, is ere, horrui, - (22) : to dread, become terrified; to bristle up; to begin to shake/tremble/shudder/shiver;

hos

hīc, haec, hoc, adj. pron. (20391) : this; these

huc

hūc, adv. (567) : here, to this place; to this point;

huius

hīc, haec, hoc, adj. pron. (20391) : this; these

hunc

hīc, haec, hoc, adj. pron. (20391) : this; these

iacet

jăcĕo, es, ere, cui, citurus (616) : to lie; to lie down; to lie ill/in ruins/prostrate/dead; to sleep; to be situated;

iactatum

jācto, as, are (300) : to throw away, throw out, throw, jerk about; to disturb; to boast, discuss; jāctātus, us, m. (3) : a throwing to and fro, a tossing

iam

jăm, jāmjăm, adv. (4207) : now, already, by/even now; besides; [non ~ => no longer; ~ pridem => long ago];

ianitor

jānītŏr, oris, m. (26) : doorkeeper, porter; janitor;

ibi

ĭbĭ, adv. (587) : there, in that place; thereupon;

ille

īllĕ, illa, illud, pron. (14503) : that; those (pl.); also DEMONST; that person/thing; the well known; the former;

illos

īllĕ, illa, illud, pron. (14503) : that; those (pl.); also DEMONST; that person/thing; the well known; the former;

imago

ĭmāgō, inis, f. (341) : likeness, image, appearance; statue; idea; echo; ghost, phantom;

imas

īnfĕrus, a, um : below, beneath, underneath; of hell; vile; lower, further down; lowest, last; īmus, a, um : inmost, deepest, bottommost, last; (inferus); [~ vox => highest treble];

immittit

īmmītto, is, ere, misi, missum (131) : to send in/to/into/against; to cause to go; to insert; to hurl/throw in; to let go/in; allow
imperium
īmpĕrĭŭm, ii, n. (1318) : command; authority; rule, supreme power; the state, the empire;
impositique
īmpōno, is, ere, sui, situm (457) : to impose, put upon; to establish; to inflict; to assign/place in command; to set;
in
ĭn, īndŭ, prép. + acc. ou + abl. (30083) : in, into, on
inceptum
īncĭpĭo, is, ere, cepi, ceptum (437) : to begin; to start, undertake;
īncēptum, i, n. (51) : a beginning, An attempt, undertaking, A purpose, subject, theme
īncēptŭs, us, m. (2) : a beginning, undertaking
inclusas
īnclūdo, is, ere, clusi, clusum (146) : to shut up/in, imprison, enclose; to include;
incolumis
īncŏlŭmĭs, e (231) : unharmed, uninjured; alive, safe; unimpaired;
increpat
īncrĕpo, is, ere, crepitum (104) : to rattle, snap, clash, roar, twang, make noise; to strike noisily;
inculta
īncūltus, a, um (60) : uncultivated (land), overgrown; unkempt; rough, uncouth; uncourted
īncŏlo, is, ere, ui, cultum (53) : to live, dwell/reside (in); to inhabit; sojourn;
inde
īndĕ, adv. (728) : thence, thenceforth; from that place/time/cause; thereupon;
īndo, is, ere, indidi, inditum (100) : to put in or on; to introduce;
indos
Īndi, orum, m. (65) : the inhabitants of India, Indians
Īndus, i, m. (11) : the name of two rivers.
Īndus, a, um (19) : Indian, from/of/belonging to India; of Indian ivory; [dens ~ => Indian ivory];
informi
īnfōrmĭs, e (29) : formless, shapeless; deformed; ugly, hideous;
ingens
īngēns, entis (679) : not natural, immoderate; huge, vast, enormous; mighty; remarkable, momentous;
ingentem
īngēns, entis (679) : not natural, immoderate; huge, vast, enormous; mighty; remarkable, momentous;
inlustris
īllūstrĭs, e (133) : bright, shining, brilliant; clear, lucid; illustrious, distinguished, famous;
innumerae
īnnŭmĕrus, a, um (27) : innumerable, countless, numberless; without number; immense;
innuptaeque
īnnūpta, ae, f. (7) : a marriage that is no marriage, an unhappy marriage
īnnūptus, a, um (7) : unmarried;
inscius
īnscĭus, a, um (41) : not knowing, ignorant; unskilled;
insidiae

73

īnsīdīāe, arum, f. pl. (321) : ambush/ambuscade (pl.); plot; treachery, treacherous attack/device; trap/snare;

insidunt

īnsīdo, is, ere, sedi, sessum (26) : to sit/settle on; to occupy/seize, hold (position); to penetrate, sink in; to merge into;

insignis

īnsīgnīs, e (217) : conspicuous, manifest, eminent, notable, famous, distinguished, outstanding;

īnsīgnē, is, n. (135) : mark, emblem, badge; ensign, honor, badge of honor;

īnsīgnĭo, is, ire, īvi (ĭi), ītum (9) : to put a mark upon, to mark; to distinguish, marked with some bodily defect, to distinguish one's self

interea

īntĕrĕā, adv. (268) : meanwhile;

invicti

īnvīctus, a, um (113) : unconquered; unconquerable, invincible;

ipse

īpsĕ, ipsa, ipsum, pron. (7890) : himself/herself/itself; the very/real/actual one; in person; themselves (pl.);

ipsius

īpsĕ, ipsa, ipsum, pron. (7890) : himself/herself/itself; the very/real/actual one; in person; themselves (pl.);

ira

īra, ae, f. (780) : anger; ire, wrath; resentment; indignation; rage/fury/violence; bad blood;

ire

ĕo, is, ire, iui, itum (1447) : to go (of every kind of motion of animate or inanimate things), to walk, ride, sail, fly, move, pass;

isque

īs, ea, id, adj. et pron. (18209) : he/she/it/they (by GENDER/NUMBER); DEMONST that, he/she/it, they/them;

ĕo, is, ire, iui, itum (1447) : to go (of every kind of motion of animate or inanimate things), to walk, ride, sail, fly, move, pass;

istinc

īstīnc, adv. (18) : from (over) there, thence; from where you are; on the other side; from here;

itala

Ĭtălus, a, um (44) : Italian;

iter

ĭtĕr, ĭtĭnĕr, itineris, n. (957) : journey; road; passage, path; march [route magnum => forced march];

ĭto, āvi, 1, intr. (2) : to go

ituras

ĕo, is, ire, iui, itum (1447) : to go (of every kind of motion of animate or inanimate things), to walk, ride, sail, fly, move, pass;

iuga

jŭgŭm, i, n. (352) : yoke; team, pair (of horses); ridge (mountain), summit, chain;

jŭgus, a, um (3) : belonging together

jŭgo, as, are (6) : to bind to laths, rails

iuli

ĭūlus, i, m. : down or woolly part of many plants, a catkin

iungere
jūngo, is, ere, iunxi, iunctum (329) : to join, unite; to bring together, clasp (hands); to connect, yoke, harness;
iuvenes
jŭvĕnĭs, is, m. (521) : youth, young man/woman;
jŭvĕnis, e (45) : the youth, the young men
lacrimae
lăcrĭma, ae, f. (516) : tear; exuded gum/sap; bit of lead; quicksilver from ore; weeping (pl.); dirge;
lacu
lăcus, us, m. (166) : basin/tank/tub; lake/pond; reservoir/cistern/basin, trough; lime-hole; bin;
laetatus
lāetŏr, aris, atus sum (126) : to be glad/joyful; to rejoic
lāeto, as, are : to be glad/joyful/delighted; to rejoice; to be fond (of), delight in; to flourish (on/in);
lapsa
lābŏr, eris, i, lapsus sum (244) : to move gently along a smooth surface, to fall, slide; to slide, slip, or glide down, to fall down, to sink (as the beginning of a fall)
lāpso, as, are (4) : to slip, slide, stumble, fall;
largo
lārgus, a, um (90) : lavish; plentiful; bountiful;
latebat
lătĕo, es, ere, latui (270) : to lie hidden, lurk; to live a retired life, escape notice;
latio
lātĭŏ, ionis, f. (3) : rendering (assistance/accounts);
latrans
lātro, as, are (35) : to bark, bark at
laxatque
lāxo, as, are (83) : to loosen, slaken, relax, weaken; to expand, open up, extend;
legere
lĕgo, is, ere, legi, lectum (619) : to read; gather, collect (cremated bones); to furl (sail), weigh (anchor); to pick out
lēgo, as, are (34) : to bequeath, will; to entrust, send as an envoy, choose as a deputy;
lethaeumque
Lēthāeus, a, um (22) : of or belonging to Lethe, Lethean
levibus
lĕvĭs, e (732) : light, thin, trivial, trifling, slight; gentle; fickle, capricious; nimble;
lēvis, e (73) : smooth, smoothed, not rough
libyae
Lĭbўa, ae, f. (29) : Libya (general term for North Africa); peoples (pl.) of Libya;
Lĭbўē, es, f. (2) : Libya
licet
lĭcĕo, v. impers. (1326) : to bid on/for, bid, bid at auction; to make a bid;
lĭcĕt, adv. conj. (183) :
lĭcĕt, licere, licuit, impers. : although, granted that; (with subjunctive);
lilia
lῑlĭum, ii, n. (23) : a lily, a reddish kind of lily
limen

līmĕn, inis, n. (269) : threshold, entrance; lintel; house;
limina
līmĕn, inis, n. (269) : threshold, entrance; lintel; house;
limo
līmus, i, m. (22) : oblique, transverse; sidelong, sideways; askew, aslant; askance;
līmus, a, um (3) : sidelong, askew, aslant, askance
locus
lŏcus, i, m. (3051) : - place, territory/locality/neighborhood/region; position/point; aim point; - part of the body; female genitals (pl.); grounds of proof;
longa
lōngus, a, um (1018) : long; tall; tedious, taking long time; boundless; far; of specific length/time;
longe
lōngē, adv. (712) : far (off), distant, a long way; by far; for a long while, far (in future/past); lōngus, a, um (1018) : long; tall; tedious, taking long time; boundless; far; of specific length/time;
longo
lōngus, a, um (1018) : long; tall; tedious, taking long time; boundless; far; of specific length/time;
lumen
lūmĕn, inis, n. (459) : light; lamp, torch; eye (of a person); life; day, daylight;
lumina
lūmĕn, inis, n. (459) : light; lamp, torch; eye (of a person); life; day, daylight;
lustrabat
lūstro, as, are (100) : to purify cermonially (w/procession), cleanse by sacrifice, expiate; to through
maeotia
Māeōtĭus, a, um (4) : Mæotian
magnanimum
māgnănĭmus, a, um (31) : brave, bold, noble in spirit (esp. kings/heroes); generous;
magnum
māgnus, a, um (6056) : - large/great/big/vast/huge; much; powerful; tall/long/broad; extensive/ - great (achievement); mighty; distinguished; skilled; bold/confident; proud; māgnŭm, adv. (6) : fortement, bruyamment, longuement
maneant
mănĕo, es, ere, mansi, mansum (609) : to remain, stay, abide; to wait for; to continue, endure, last; to spend the night
manu
mănŭs, us, f. (2540) : hand, fist; team; gang, band of soldiers; handwriting; (elephant's) trunk;
manus
mănŭs, us, f. (2540) : hand, fist; team; gang, band of soldiers; handwriting; (elephant's) trunk;
mānus, a, um (3) : i. q. bonus
manusque
mănŭs, us, f. (2540) : hand, fist; team; gang, band of soldiers; handwriting; (elephant's) trunk;
mānus, a, um (3) : i. q. bonus

matres
mătĕr, tris, f. (992) : mother, foster mother; lady, matron; origin, source, motherland, mother city;
mea
mĕus, mea, meum (1116) : my (personal possession); mine, of me, belonging to me; my own; to me;
mĕum, i, n. (10) : mine, my property, my daughter, it is my affair, my concern, my duty, my custom
mĕo, as, are (35) : go along, pass, travel;
medios
mĕdĭus, a, um (870) : middle, middle of, mid; common, neutral, ordinary, moderate; ambiguous;
memorans
mĕmŏro, as, are (237) : to remember; to be mindful of (w/GEN/ACC); to mention/recount/relate, remind/speak of;
mento
mĕntŭm, i, n. (24) : chin; projecting edge (architecture);
metui
mĕtŭo, is, ere, ui, utum (504) : to fear; to be afraid; to stand in fear of; to be apprehensive, dread;
mĕtus, us, m. (986) : fear, anxiety; dread, awe; object of awe/dread;
ministrat
mĭnīstro, as, are (65) : attend (to), serve, furnish; supply;
moresque
mōs, moris, m. (1227) : custom, habit; mood, manner, fashion; character (pl.), behavior, morals;
moveri
mŏvĕo, es, ere, moui, motum (858) : to move, stir, agitate, affect, provoke, disturb; [movere se => dance];
movet
mŏvĕo, es, ere, moui, motum (858) : to move, stir, agitate, affect, provoke, disturb; [movere se => dance];
multa
mūltus, a, um (4547) : much, many, great; large, intense, assiduous; tedious;
mūltum, i, n. (206) : grande quantité
mūlta, mūlcta, ae, f. (37) : fine; penalty; penalty involving property (livestock, later money);
mūlto, as, are (33) : to punish, to punish with his vows, by granting the object of his vows
multae
mūltus, a, um (4547) : much, many, great; large, intense, assiduous; tedious;
mūlta, mūlcta, ae, f. (37) : fine; penalty; penalty involving property (livestock, later money);
multam
mūltus, a, um (4547) : much, many, great; large, intense, assiduous; tedious;
mūlta, mūlcta, ae, f. (37) : fine; penalty; penalty involving property (livestock, later money);
murmure
mūrmŭr, uris, n. (88) : murmur/mutter; whisper/rustle, hum/buzz; low noise; roar/growl/grunt/rumble;
nate

nātus, i, m. (318) : born, arisen; made; destined; designed, intended, produced by nature; aged,

nătĭs, is, f. (6) : the rump, buttocks

nō, as, are (43) : to swim, float;

nāscŏr, eris, i, natus sum (502) : to be born, to be begotten

nătus, a, um (76) : born;

natumque

nātus, i, m. (318) : born, arisen; made; destined; designed, intended, produced by nature; aged,

nāscŏr, eris, i, natus sum (502) : to be born, to be begotten

nātŭs, us, m. (53) : birth;

nătus, a, um (76) : born;

nō, as, are (43) : to swim, float;

navita

nāvĭta, ae, m. (46) : sailor, seaman, mariner; (early, late, and poetic);

nec

něc, adv. (6689) : nor, and..not; not..either, not even;

nefas

něfās, n. (188) : sin, violation of divine law, impious act; [fas et nefas => right and wrong];

nemus

němŭs, oris, n. (246) : wood, forest;

nepotes

něpōs, otis, m. (174) : grandson/daughter; descendant; spendthrift, prodigal, playboy; secondary shoot;

nili

nīlus, i, m. : un aqueduc

nīlum, i, n. : nothing

nīlĭŏs, ii, f. : a precious stone, of the color of a dark topaz

nocerent

nŏcěo, es, ere, nocui, nocitum (410) : to harm, hurt; to injure (with DAT);

noctisque

nōx, noctis, f. (1104) : night [prima nocte => early in the night; multa nocte => late at night];

nodo

nōdus, i, m. (73) : knot; node;

nōdo, as, are (5) : to furnish, fill with knots

nomen

nōměn, inis, n. (2073) : name, family name; noun; account, entry in debt ledger; sake; title, heading;

nostro

nōstěr, tra, trum, adj. pron. (2823) : our;

nostrumque

nōstěr, tra, trum, adj. pron. (2823) : our;

nōs, nostrum pron. pl. (3244) : we (pl.), us;

notas

nŏto, as, are (180) : to observe; to record; to brand; to write, inscribe;

nŏta, ae, f. (186) : mark, sign, letter, word, writing, spot brand, tattoo-mark;

nōtus, a, um (430) : well known, familiar, notable, famous, esteemed; notorious, of ill repute;

nōsco, is, ere, noui, notum (554) : to get to know; to learn, find out; to become cognizant of/acquainted/familiar with;
nulla
nūllŭs, a, um (2757) : no; none, not any; (PRONominal ADJ)
nullae
nūllŭs, a, um (2757) : no; none, not any; (PRONominal ADJ)
numerum
nŭmĕrus, i, m. (809) : - number/sum/total/rank; (superior) numerical strength/plurality; category; - rhythm/cadence/frequency; meter/metrical foot/line; melody; exercise
nunc
nūnc, adv. (3149) : now, today, at present;
occurrens
ōccūrro, is, ere, curri, cursum (335) : to run to meet; to oppose, resist; to come to mind, occur (with DAT);
omnem
ōmnĭs, e (2203) : all men (pl.), all persons;
omnemque
ōmnĭs, e (2203) : all men (pl.), all persons;
omnis
ōmnĭs, e (2203) : all men (pl.), all persons;
ōmne, is, n. : every thing
ora
ōs, oris, n. (958) : the mouth; the face, countenance; A mouth, opening, entrance, aperture, orifice;
ōra, ae, f. (226) : shore, coast;
ōro, as, are (385) : to burn;
orantes
ōro, as, are (385) : to burn;
ordine
ōrdō, inis, m. (899) : row, order/rank; succession; series; class; bank (oars); order (of monks)
ore
ōs, oris, n. (958) : the mouth; the face, countenance; A mouth, opening, entrance, aperture, orifice;
ostia
ōstĭŭm, ii, n. (75) : doorway; front door; starting gate; entrance (underworld); (river) mouth;
palmas
pālma, ae, f. (134) : palm/width of the hand; hand; palm tree/branch; date; palm award/first place;
paludem
pălūs, udis, f. (134) : swamp, marsh;
par
pār, paris (718) : - equal (to); a match for; of equal size/rank/age; fit/suitable/right/proper; - corresponding in degree, proportionate, commensurate (unlike qualities); - balanced/level;
pār, păris, n. (33) : a pair
pār, păris, m. (6) : a companion, comrade, mate, spouse
parenti
pārēns, entis, comm. (681) : -I. obedient -II. a subject

pārĕo, pārrĕo, es, ere, ui, itum (307) : - to obey, be subject/obedient to; to submit/yield/comply; to pay attention; to attend to;
părēns, entis, m. (3) : obedient;

parentum

pārĕo, pārrĕo, es, ere, ui, itum (307) : - to obey, be subject/obedient to; to submit/yield/comply; to pay attention; to attend to;
părēns, entis, m. (3) : obedient;

pater

pătĕr, tris, m. (2272) : father; [pater familias, patris familias => head of family/household];

patrui

pătrŭus, i, m. (99) : "- father's brother; paternal uncle; [~ magnus/major/maximus => gr/gr-gr/gr-gr- - severe reprover; type of harshness/censoriousness/finding fault; ""Dutch" pătrŭus, a, um (3) : of or belonging to a father's brother, of an uncle, an uncle's, sup.

pedemque

pēs, pedis, m. (811) : foot; [pedem referre => to retreat];
pēdĭs, is, comm. (2) : a louse

penitus

pĕnĭtŭs, (penite) adv. (166) : inside; deep within; thoroughly;

peragunt

pĕrăgo, is, ere, egi, actum (153) : to disturb; to finish; to kill; to carry through to the end, complete;

periclis

pĕrīcŭlŭm, pĕrīclŭm, i, n. (1235) : danger, peril; trial, attempt; risk; responsibility for damage, liability;

petivit

pēto, is, ere, iui, itum (1865) : to attack; to aim at; to desire; to beg, entreat, ask (for); to reach towards, make for;

pietas

pīĕtās, atis, f. (274) : responsibility, sense of duty; loyalty; tenderness, goodness; pity; piety

pietate

pīĕtās, atis, f. (274) : responsibility, sense of duty; loyalty; tenderness, goodness; pity; piety

pietatis

pīĕtās, atis, f. (274) : responsibility, sense of duty; loyalty; tenderness, goodness; pity; piety

pirithoumque

Pīrīthŏus, i, m. (10) : son of Ixion, king of the Lapithœ, husband of Hippodamia, and friend of Theseus. After the death of Hippodamia, he descended, in company with Theseus, to the infernal regions, to carry away Proserpine; but was, together with Theseus, seized and detained in chains. Theseus was afterwards delivered by Hercules, who vainly endeavored to save Pirithoüs also

placidas

plăcĭdus, a, um (183) : gentle, calm, mild, peaceful, placid;

plura

mūltus, a, um (4547) : much, many, great; large, intense, assiduous; tedious;

plurima

mūltus, a, um (4547) : much, many, great; large, intense, assiduous; tedious;
plūrĭmus, a, um : most, greatest number/amount; very many; most frequent; highest price/value;

pondere

pŏndŭs, eris, n. (305) : weight, burden, impediment;
pontum
pŏntus, i, m. (149) : sea;
populique
pŏpŭlus, pŏplus, i, m. (2558) : people, nation, State; public/populace/multitude/crowd; a following
pōpŭlus, i, f. (23) : poplar tree; (long o)
porro
pŏrrō, adv. (233) : at distance, further on, far off, onward; of old, formerly, hereafter; again;
pŏrrŭm, i, m. (6) : leek;
pŏrrus, i, m. (4) : a leek, scallion;, chives
portitor
pŏrtĭtŏr, oris, m. (11) : ferry man;
posset
pŏssŭm, potes, posse, potui (9115) : to be able, can; [multum posse => have much/more/most influence/power];
post
pŏst, adv, prép. + acc. (1274) : behind (space), after (time); subordinate to (rank);
praenatat
prāenăto, as, are (3) : To swim before, in front
pratis
prātŭm, i, n. (80) : meadow, meadowland; meadow grass/crop; broad expanse/field/plain (land/sea);
primi
prīmus, a, um (1719) : first, foremost/best, chief, principal; nearest/next
primo
prīmus, a, um (1719) : first, foremost/best, chief, principal; nearest/next
prīmō, adv. : at first; in the first place; at the beginning;
prior
prĭŏr, oris (458) : superior/elder monk; (later) second in dignity to abbot/head of priory, prior;
proferet
prōfĕro, fers, ferre, tuli, latum (342) : to bring forward; to advance; to defer; to discover; to mention;
progenies
prōgĕnĭes, ei, f. (40) : race, family, progeny;
prolem
prōlēs, is, f. (105) : offspring, descendant; that springs by birth/descent; generation; race, breed;
promitti
prōmītto, is, ere, misi, missum (344) : to promise;
propinquant
prŏpīnquo, as, are (35) : to bring near; to draw near;
propinquat
prŏpīnquo, as, are (35) : to bring near; to draw near;
proserpina
Prŏsērpīna, ae, f. (17) : Proserpine
prospexit

prōspǐcǐo, is, ere, spexi, spectum (160) : to foresee; to see far off; to watch for, provide for, look out for;

puellae

pǔēlla, ae, f. (561) : girl, (female) child/daughter; maiden; young woman/wife; sweetheart; slavegirl;

pueri

pǔěr, eri, m. (882) : boy, lad, young man; servant; (male) child; [a puere => from boyhood];

puppim

pūppis, pūppes, is, f. (45) : stern/aft (of ship); poop; ship; back

quae

quī, quae, quod, pron. rel. (41601) : who; that; which, what; of which kind/degree; person/thing/time/point that

quǐs, quae, quid, pron. interr. (13642) : who? which? what? what man?

quam

quǎm, quāmdě, quāndě, adv. (5587) : how, than;

quī, quae, quod, pron. rel. (41601) : who; that; which, what; of which kind/degree; person/thing/time/point that

quǐs, quae, quid, pron. interr. (13642) : who? which? what? what man?

quamquam

quāmquǎm, quānquǎm, conj. sub. + ind. (485) : though, although; yet; nevertheless;

quīsquǎm, quaequam, quidquam ou quic- (1051) : any, any one, any body, any thing, something

quanta

quāntus, a, um, adj., pron. excl et interr (789) : how great; how much/many; of what size/amount/degree/number/worth/price;

quantis

quāntus, a, um, adj., pron. excl et interr (789) : how great; how much/many; of what size/amount/degree/number/worth/price;

quas

quī, quae, quod, pron. rel. (41601) : who; that; which, what; of which kind/degree; person/thing/time/point that

quǐs, quae, quid, pron. interr. (13642) : who? which? what? what man?

quem

quī, quae, quod, pron. rel. (41601) : who; that; which, what; of which kind/degree; person/thing/time/point that

quǐs, quae, quid, pron. interr. (13642) : who? which? what? what man?

quid

quǐs, quae, quid, pron. interr. (13642) : who? which? what? what man?

quǐd, adv. interr. : how? why? wherefore?

quisquis

quīsquǐs, quidquid ou quicquid (641) : whoever, whosoever, whatever, whatsoever, every one who, each, every, all

quive

quī, quae, quod, pron. rel. (41601) : who; that; which, what; of which kind/degree; person/thing/time/point that

quǐs, quae, quid, pron. interr. (13642) : who? which? what? what man?

quī, adv. (193) : how?; how so; in what way; by what/which means; whereby; at whatever price;

quĕo, is, ire, ii ou iui, itum (191) : to be able;
quondam
quōndăm, adv. (288) : un jour, à un certain moment, autrefois
quos
quī, quae, quod, pron. rel. (41601) : who; that; which, what; of which kind/degree; person/thing/time/point that
quĭs, quae, quid, pron. interr. (13642) : who? which? what? what man?
ramum
rāmus, i, m. (168) : branch, bough;
ratem
rătĭs, is, f. (204) : raft; ship, boat;
rebarque
rĕŏr, reris, reri, ratus sum (232) : to think, regard; to deem; to suppose, believe, reckon
recensebat
rĕcēnsĕo, es, ere, censui, censum (16) : to review/examine/survey/muster; to enumerate/count, make census/roll; to pass in
recolens
rĕcōlo, is, ere, colui, cultum (11) : to cultivate afresh; to go over in one's mind;
reddere
rēddo, is, ere, ddidi, dditum (1102) : to return; to restore; to deliver; to hand over, pay back, render, give back; to translate;
reducta
rĕdūco, is, ere, duxi, ductum (188) : to lead back, bring back; to restore; to reduce;
rĕdūctus, a, um (6) : withdrawn, retired, remote, distant, lonely, withdrawn, removed, remote, from either extreme, n, things to be deferred to others
regis
rēx, regis, m. (2196) : king;
rĕgo, is, ere, rexi, rectum (296) : to rule, guide; to manage, direct;
rēgĭa, ae, f. (131) : palace, court; residence;
rēgĭus, a, um (300) : royal, of a king, regal;
regna
rēgnŭm, i, n. (907) : royal power; power; control; kingdom;
rēgno, as, are (152) : reign, rule; be king; play the lord, be master;
regnata
rēgno, as, are (152) : reign, rule; be king; play the lord, be master;
requirit
rĕquīro, is, ere, i, quisitum (199) : to require, seek, ask for; to need; to miss, pine for;
residunt
rĕsīdo, is, ere, sēdi, sessum, intr. (46) : to sit down, to settle
responsis
rēspōndĕo, es, ere, di, sum (659) : to answer;
rēspōnsŭm, i, n. (112) : answer, response;
rigabat
rīgo, as, are (41) : to moisten, wet, water, irrigate;
rimosa
rīmōsus, a, um (7) : full of cracks, chinks, fissures
ripae
rīpa, ae, f. (269) : bank;

ripaeque
rīpa, ae, f. (269) : bank;
ripas
rīpa, ae, f. (269) : bank;
rogis
rŏgus, i, m. (103) : funeral pyre;
romanosque
Rōmānus, a, um (2392) : Roman, a Roman
Rōmāni, orum, m. (262) : les Romains
Rōmānus, i, m. (8) : Sing. collect., = the Romans; a Roman
ruebat
rŭo, is, ere, rui, rutum (248) : to destroy, ruin, overthrow; to rush on, run; to fall; to charge (in + ACC); to be ruined;
rursus
rūrsŭs, adv. (414) : turned back, backward; on the contrary/other hand, in return, in turn, again;
saecula
sāecŭlŭm, i, n. (190) : time; past/present/future (Plater); [in ~ => forever];
saepius
sāepĕ, adv. (1507) : often, oft, oftimes, many times, frequently;
sale
sāl, salis, m. (89) : salt; wit; the sea
sălĕ, is, n. (3) : salt
saturno
Sātūrnus, i, m. (54) : Saturn; according to the myth, the most ancient king of Latium, who came to Italy in the reign of Janus
seclusum
sēclūdo, is, ere, clusi, clusum (9) : to shut off, shut in a separate place, to shut up, seclude
sed
sĕd, conj. (9689) : but, but also; yet; however, but in fact/truth; not to mention; yes but;
sedebant
sēdĕo, es, ere, sedi, sessum (373) : to sit, remain; to settle; to encamp;
senectus
sĕnēctūs, utis, f. (300) : old age; extreme age; senility; old men; gray hairs; shed snake skin;
sĕnēctus, a, um (7) : very old, aged
senior
sĕnēx, sĕnis (146) : old, aged, advanced in years
sĕnĭŏr, oris, m. (43) : older/elderly man, senior; (in Rome a man over 45);
senus, a, um, cf. seni (12) : six each
septemgemini
sēptēmgĕmĭnus, a, um (3) : sevenfold
sequatur
sĕquŏr, eris, i, secutus sum (1274) : to follow; to escort/attend/accompany; to aim at/reach after/strive for/make for/seek
serena
sĕrēnus, a, um (49) : clear, fair, bright; serene, tranquil; cheerful, glad;
sĕrēnum, i, n. (14) : temps serein
sĕrēno, as, are (4) : to make clear, fair, serene, to clear up

servat
sērvo, as, are (708) : to watch over; to protect, store, keep, guard, preserve, save;
servet
sērvo, as, are (708) : to watch over; to protect, store, keep, guard, preserve, save;
sibyllam
Sībȳlla, Sībūlla, ae, f. (23) : prophetess, sibyl;
sic
sīc, sĕic, adv. (2237) : ainsi (... ut, ainsi que)
sidera
sīdŭs, ĕris, n. (339) : star; constellation; tempest (Vulgate 4 Ezra 15,39);
silvae
sīlva, ae, f. (493) : wood, forest (sylvan);
silvis
sīlva, ae, f. (493) : wood, forest (sylvan);
simillima
sĭmīlĭs, e (597) : like, similar, resembling;
simul
sĭmŭl, sĕmŭl, adv. (906) : en même temps, [conj.] dès que
sint
sŭm, es, esse, fui (40916) : to be; to exist; (also used to form verb perfect passive tenses) with NOM PERF PPL
solio
sŏlĭŭm, ii, n. (52) : throne, seat;
solisque
sŏl, solis, m. (513) : sun;
sŏlŭm, i, n. (264) : only/just/merely/barely/alone;
sŏlĭŭm, ii, n. (52) : throne, seat;
sŏlus, a, um (91) : only, single; lonely; alone, having no companion/friend/protector; unique;
somni
sōmnus, i, m. (406) : sleep;
sōmnĭŭm, ii, n. (66) : dream, vision; fantasy, day-dream;
somno
sōmnus, i, m. (406) : sleep;
sonantem
sŏno, as, are, sonui, sonitum (192) : - to make a noise/sound; speak/utter, emit sound; to be spoken of (as); to express - to echo/resound; to be heard, sound; to be spoken of (as); to celebrate in speech;
sŏnāns, antis (18) : sounding, resounding, resonant
sonantia
sŏno, as, are, sonui, sonitum (192) : - to make a noise/sound; speak/utter, emit sound; to be spoken of (as); to express - to echo/resound; to be heard, sound; to be spoken of (as); to celebrate in speech;
sŏnāns, antis (18) : sounding, resounding, resonant
soporae
sŏpōrus, a, um (2) : of or belonging to sleep
sordidus
sōrdĭdus, a, um (160) : dirty, unclean, foul, filthy; vulgar, sordid; low, base, mean, paltry; vile;
squalore

squālŏr, oris, m. (45) : squalor, filth;

stabant

stō, as, are, steti, statum (843) : to stand, stand still, stand firm; to remain, rest;

stant

stō, as, are, steti, statum (843) : to stand, stand still, stand firm; to remain, rest;

stellis

stēlla, ae, f. (81) : star; planet, heavenly body; point of light in jewel; constellation; star

strepit

strĕpo, is, ere, strepui, strepitum (33) : to make a loud noise; to shout confusedly; to resound;

studio

stŭdĭŭm, ii, n. (958) : eagerness, enthusiasm, zeal, spirit; devotion, pursuit, study;

stygia

Stȳgĭus, a, um (59) : Stygian, of river Styx; of fountain Styx;

sub

sŭb, prép. + acc. / abl. (1055) : under; up to, up under, close to (of motion); until, before, up to, about;

subigit

sŭbĭgo, is, ere, egi, actum (112) : to conquer, subjugate; to compel;

subito

sŭbĭtō, adv. (300) : suddenly, unexpectedly; at once, at short notice, quickly; in no time at all;
sŭbĭtus, a, um (208) : sudden; rash, unexpected;
sŭbĭtum, i, n. (12) : a sudden, unexpected thing, a sudden occurrence, whether he spoke after deliberation, off-hand
sŭbĕo, is, ire, ii, itum (329) : - to go/move/pass/sink/extend underneath/into; to climb/come/go up, ascend; to steal in - to place/be placed under/in support; to come up w/aid; to assume a form; to undergo;

subtrahe

sŭbtrăho, is, ere, traxi, tractum (58) : to carry off; to take away; to subtract;

subvectat

sŭbvēcto, as, are (6) : to convey (often or laboriously) upwards;

sum

sŭm, es, esse, fui (40916) : to be; to exist; (also used to form verb perfect passive tenses) with NOM PERF PPL

summotos

sŭbmŏvĕo, es, ere, moui, motum (86) : to remove; to drive off, dislodge; to expel; to ward off; to keep at a distance; to bar/debar;

suorum

sŭus, a, um, adj. et pron. (7170) : his/one's (own), her (own), hers, its (own); (pl.) their (own), theirs;
sŭum, i, n. (154) : (et surtout pl. sua) son bien, ses biens, leurs biens

super

sŭpĕr, prép. + acc. / abl. (405) : upon/on; over, above, about; besides (space); during (time); beyond (degree);
sŭpĕr, era, erum cf. superus (44) : above, high; higher, upper, of this world; greatest, last, highest;

superumque

sŭpĕr, era, erum cf. superus (44) : above, high; higher, upper, of this world; greatest, last, highest;

sŭpĕrus, a, um : above, high; higher, upper, of this world; greatest, last, highest;

sutilis

sūtĭlĭs, e (4) : sewed together, bound, fastened together

tacitum

tăcĕo, es, ere, cui, citum (337) : to be silent; to pass over in silence; to leave unmentioned, be silent about something;

tăcītus, a, um (234) : silent, secret;

tăcītum, i, n. (5) : -I. a secret -II. silence

tales

tālĭs, e (441) : such; so great; so excellent; of such kind;

tandem

tāndĕm, adv. (473) : finally; at last, in the end; after some time, eventually; at length;

tantae

tāntus, a, um (506) : of such size; so great, so much; [tantus ... quantus => as much ... as];

tanto

tāntō, adv. (193) : (suivi d'un comparatif) autant, d'autant

tāntus, a, um (506) : of such size; so great, so much; [tantus ... quantus => as much ... as];

tartarei

Tārtărĕus, a, um (18) : of or belonging to the underworld; Tartarean;

tartareum

Tārtărĕus, a, um (18) : of or belonging to the underworld; Tartarean;

te

tū, tui, sing. pron. (13016) : you (sing.); thou/thine/thee/thy (PERS); yourself/thyself (REFLEX);

tela

tēlŭm, i, n. (761) : dart, spear; weapon, javelin; bullet (gun);

tēla, ae, f. (29) : web; warp (threads that run lengthwise in the loom);

tellus

tēllūs, uris, f. (310) : earth, ground; the earth; land, country;

tempora

tēmpŭs, oris, n. (2770) : time, condition, right time; season, occasion; necessity;

tempore

tēmpŭs, oris, n. (2770) : time, condition, right time; season, occasion; necessity;

tendebantque

tēndo, is, ere, tetendi, tensum (283) : - to stretch/spread/extend; to distend; to aim/direct weapon/glance/steps/course; - to pitch tent, encamp; to pull tight; to draw (bow); to press on, insist; to exert oneself;

tendentem

tēndo, is, ere, tetendi, tensum (283) : - to stretch/spread/extend; to distend; to aim/direct weapon/glance/steps/course; - to pitch tent, encamp; to pull tight; to draw (bow); to press on, insist; to exert oneself;

tendere

tēndo, is, ere, tetendi, tensum (283) : - to stretch/spread/extend; to distend; to aim/direct weapon/glance/steps/course; - to pitch tent, encamp; to pull tight; to draw (bow); to press on, insist; to exert oneself;

tendis

tēndo

tēndo, is, ere, tetendi, tensum (283) : - to stretch/spread/extend; to distend; to aim/direct weapon/glance/steps/course; - to pitch tent, encamp; to pull tight; to draw (bow); to press on, insist; to exert oneself;

teque

tū, tui, sing. pron. (13016) : you (sing.); thou/thine/thee/thy (PERS); yourself/thyself (REFLEX);

ter

tĕr, adv. (196) : three times; on three occasions;

terram

tērra, ae, f. (1737) : earth, land, ground; country, region;

terras

tērra, ae, f. (1737) : earth, land, ground; country, region;

terreat

tērrĕo, es, ere, ui, itum (259) : to frighten, scare, terrify, deter;

terribili

tērrĭbĭlĭs, e (67) : frightful, terrible;

terris

tērra, ae, f. (1737) : earth, land, ground; country, region;

tetendit

tēndo, is, ere, tetendi, tensum (283) : - to stretch/spread/extend; to distend; to aim/direct weapon/glance/steps/course; - to pitch tent, encamp; to pull tight; to draw (bow); to press on, insist; to exert oneself;

thalamo

thălămus, i, m. (133) : bedroom; marriage;

thesea

Thēsēus, i, m. (76) : a king of Athens, son of Ægeus, of Neptune, and Aethra;
Thēsēus, a, um (8) : of or belonging to Theseus, Thesean, Athenian

tibi

tū, tui, sing. pron. (13016) : you (sing.); thou/thine/thee/thy (PERS); yourself/thyself (REFLEX);

torquet

tōrquĕo, es, ere, torsi, tortum (267) : to turn, twist; to hurl; to torture; to torment; to bend, distort; spin, whirl; to wind (round);

trahit

trăho, is, ere, traxi, tractum (590) : to draw, drag, haul; to derive, get;

trans

trāns, prép. + acc. (81) : across, over; beyond; on the other side; (only local relations);

transmittere

trānsmītto, trāmītto, is, ere, misi, missum (55) : to send across; to go across; to transmit;

traxitque

trăho, is, ere, traxi, tractum (590) : to draw, drag, haul; to derive, get;

trementem

trĕmo, is, ere, ui, - (153) : to tremble, shake, shudder at;
trĕmēns, entis : temblant

trepida

trĕpĭdus, a, um (144) : nervous, jumpy, agitated; perilous, alarming, frightened; boiling, foaming;
trĕpĭdo, as, are (125) : to tremble, be afraid, waver;

tristis
trīstīs, e (518) : sad, sorrowful; gloomy;
trīste, is, n. (6) : a sad thing
troius
Trōĭus, a, um (27) : of Troy, Trojan
tua
tŭus, a, um (3630) : your (sing.);
tuaque
tŭus, a, um (3630) : your (sing.);
tueri
tŭĕŏr, eris, eri, tuitus sum (404) : to look at; to protect, watch; uphold
tum
tŭm, adv. (2556) : moreover; (frequent in Cicero and before; rare after);
tumida
tŭmĭdus, a, um (101) : swollen, swelling, distended; puffed up with pride or self; confidence;
tumulum
tŭmŭlus, i, m. (138) : mound, hillock; mound, tomb;
tuos
tŭus, a, um (3630) : your (sing.);
turba
tūrba, ae, f. (489) : commotion, uproar, turmoil, tumult, disturbance; crowd, mob, multitude;
tūrbo, as, are (205) : to disturb, agitate, confuse, disorder; to throw into disorder or confusion
turbamque
tūrba, ae, f. (489) : commotion, uproar, turmoil, tumult, disturbance; crowd, mob, multitude;
turbant
tūrbo, as, are (205) : to disturb, agitate, confuse, disorder; to throw into disorder or confusion
turbidus
tūrbĭdus, a, um (103) : - wild/stormy; muddy/turbid; murky/foggy/clouded/opaque; gloomy, frowning;
tyrrheno
Tўrrhēnus, a, um (47) : of or belonging to the Tyrrhenians, Etrurians, Tyrrhenian, Etrurian,
Tuscan
Tўrrhēnus, i, m. (4) : of or belonging to the Tyrrhenians or Etrurians, Tyrrhenian, Etrurian, Tuscan
ubi
ŭbĭ, adv. interr. ou rel. (956) : where, whereby;
ulterioris
ūltĕrĭŏr, oris (63) : farther, on the farther side, that is beyond, ulterior
ūltĕrĭōra, um, n. (8) : the more remote parts or regions, the districts beyond
ultro
ūltrŏ̆, adv. (270) : voluntarily, of one's own accord
ulua
ūlva, ae, f. (9) : sedge; (collective term) various grass/rush-like aquatic plants;
umbrarum
ūmbra, ae, f. (387) : shade; ghost; shadow;
umbras
ūmbra, ae, f. (387) : shade; ghost; shadow;

ūmbro, as, are (6) : to shade, shadow, overshadow, overspread, cover; to make, cast a shade

umeris
ūmĕrus, i, m. (193) : upper arm, shoulder;
ūmĕo, es, ere (14) : to be wet; to be moist;

umero
ūmĕrus, i, m. (193) : upper arm, shoulder;

unaque
ūnus, a, um, sing. (3148) : alone, a single/sole; some, some one; only (pl.); one set of (denoting entity);
ūnā, adv. (281) : together, together with; at the same time; along with;

unda
ūnda, ae, f. (511) : wave;
ūndo, as, are (15) : to surge/flood/rise in waves; to gush/well up; to run, stream; to billow; to undulate; to waver;

undas
ūnda, ae, f. (511) : wave;
ūndo, as, are (15) : to surge/flood/rise in waves; to gush/well up; to run, stream; to billow; to undulate; to waver;

unde
ūndĕ, adv. interr. ou rel. (418) : from where, whence, from what or which place; from which; from whom;

ut
ŭt, ŭtŭt, conj. sub. + ind. ou subj. (10753) : to (+ subjunctive), in order that/to; how, as, when, while; even if;

utrasque
ūtērque, utraque, utrumque (769) : each, either, each one, one and the other, one as well as the other, both

valle
vāllēs, is, f. (113) : a valley, vale.
vāllīs, is, f. (9) : valley, vale, hollow;

variis
vărĭŭs, a, um (404) : different; various, diverse; changing; colored; party colored, variegated;

vastaque
vāstus, a, um (222) : huge, vast; monstrous;
vāsto, as, are (89) : to lay waste, ravage, devastate;

vatemque
vātēs, is, m. (215) : prophet/seer, mouthpiece of deity; oracle, soothsayer; poet (divinely
vātīs, is, m. : prophetess/ mouthpiece of deity; oracle/soothsayer; poetess (divinely

vates
vātēs, is, m. (215) : prophet/seer, mouthpiece of deity; oracle, soothsayer; poet (divinely
vātīs, is, m. : prophetess/ mouthpiece of deity; oracle/soothsayer; poetess (divinely

vectare
vēcto, as, are (16) : to transport, carry; (of habitual agent/means); (PASS) to ride, be conveyed, travel;

vectum
vĕho, is, ere, uexi, uectum (238) : to bear, carry, convey; to pass, ride, sail;

velisque

vēlŭm, i, n. (203) : sail, covering; curtain; [vela vento dare => sail away];
veluti
vĕlŭtī, adv. (77) : just as, as if;
venerabile
vĕnĕrābĭlĭs, e (23) : venerable, august;
venias
vĕnĭo, is, ire, ueni, uentum (2796) : to come;
vĕnĭa, ae, f. (199) : favor, kindness; pardon; permission; indulgence;
venientum
vĕnĭo, is, ire, ueni, uentum (2796) : to come;
venisti
vĕnĭo, is, ire, ueni, uentum (2796) : to come;
vēnĕo, is, ire, īvi (ii), ĭtum, intr. (132) : to go to sale, to be sold
ventis
vĕnĭo, is, ire, ueni, uentum (2796) : to come;
vĕntus, i, m. (586) : wind;
ventura
vĕnĭo, is, ire, ueni, uentum (2796) : to come;
vero
vērō, adv. (557) : yes; in truth; certainly; truly, to be sure; however;
vērus, a, um (605) : true, real, genuine, actual; properly named; well founded; right, fair, proper;
veste
vēstĭs, is, f. (438) : garment, clothing, blanket; clothes; robe;
via
vĭa, ae, f. (822) : way, road, street; journey;
vias
vĭa, ae, f. (822) : way, road, street; journey;
vicit
vīnco, is, ere, uici, uictum (1102) : to conquer, defeat, excel; to outlast; to succeed;
videt
vĭdĕo, es, ere, uidi, uisum (6605) : to see, look at; to consider; (PASS) to seem, seem good, appear, be seen;
vidit
vĭdĕo, es, ere, uidi, uisum (6605) : to see, look at; to consider; (PASS) to seem, seem good, appear, be seen;
vim
vīs, -, f. (2188) : strength (bodily) (pl.), force, power, might, violence; resources; large body;
vincla
vīnclŭm, i, n. (138) : chain, bond, fetter; imprisonment (pl.);
vir
vĭr, uiri, m. (2702) : man; husband; hero; person of courage, honor, and nobility;
virenti
vĭrēns, entis (16) : plants (pl.); herbage;
vĭrĕo, es, ere (30) : to be green or verdant; to be lively or vigorous; to be full of youthful vigor;
virgae
vīrga, ae, f. (94) : twig, sprout, stalk; switch, rod; staff, wand; stripe/streak; scepter (Plater);
virgulta

vīrgūltus, a, um : full of bushes, thickets, shrubby

viri

vĭr, uiri, m. (2702) : man; husband; hero; person of courage, honor, and nobility;

vīrus, i, n. (34) : a slimy liquid, slime.

viribus

vīs, -, f. (2188) : strength (bodily) (pl.), force, power, might, violence; resources; large body;

viridisque

vĭrĭdĭs, e (125) : fresh, green; blooming,youthful;

vĭrĭde, is, n. (3) : Green color, greenness, verdure

virum

vĭr, uiri, m. (2702) : man; husband; hero; person of courage, honor, and nobility;

virumque

vĭr, uiri, m. (2702) : man; husband; hero; person of courage, honor, and nobility;

visu

vīsus, us, m. (75) : look, sight, appearance; vision;

vĭdĕo, es, ere, uidi, uisum (6605) : to see, look at; to consider; (PASS) to seem, seem good, appear, be seen;

vīso, is, ere, uisi, uisum (161) : to visit, go to see; to look at;

visum

vĭdĕo, es, ere, uidi, uisum (6605) : to see, look at; to consider; (PASS) to seem, seem good, appear, be seen;

vīso, is, ere, uisi, uisum (161) : to visit, go to see; to look at;

vīsus, us, m. (75) : look, sight, appearance; vision;

vīsum, i, n. (17) : something seen, sight, appearance, vision.

vita

vīta, ae, f. (2080) : life, career, livelihood; mode of life;

vīto, as, are (260) : to avoid, shun; to evade;

viva

vīvus, a, um (257) : alive, fresh; living;

voces

vōx, uocis, f. (1171) : voice, tone, expression;

volabant

vŏlo, as, are (135) : to fly

volucrique

vŏlŭcrīs, is, f. (85) : bird, flying insect/creature; constellation Cycnus/Cygnus;

voragine

vŏrāgō, inis, f. (21) : deep hole, chasm, watery hollow;

vox

vōx, uocis, f. (1171) : voice, tone, expression;

vultus

vūltus, vōltus, us, m. (448) : face, expression; looks;

Printed in Great Britain
by Amazon